CW00550748

Respect

Stories of troubled children in an
alternative educational provision

by

Dominic Boddington MBE
Liz Easton

Copyright © 2021 Dominic Boddington
Liz Easton

ISBN: 9798598766927

All rights reserved, including the right to reproduce this book, or portions thereof in any form. No part of this text may be reproduced, transmitted, downloaded, decompiled, reverse engineered, or stored, in any form or introduced into any information storage and retrieval system, in any form or by any means, whether electronic or mechanical without the express written permission of the author.

This immensely readable book has gripping stories that filled me with both horror and hope. Horror that so many of our young people are falling through the gaps and that we have an education system that simply does not meet their needs. And hope that there are people like those at Respect who care about these kids and have the skills to intervene and often change the narrative of young lives. The challenges of this task are laid bare , not just in the young people themselves but in a system that continues to marginalise the most vulnerable in our society. Schools must be more than test-driven academies and as this book illustrates over and over again - understanding and empathic relationships change everything.

Dr. Sue Roffey, teacher, educational psychologist, academic and author of many books about behaviour, relationships in schools and the craft of teaching.

I loved the atmosphere of the book, the vividly drawn characters, the high jinks, cajoling young people from their beds, hooking them into activities, sharing their pain and joy. Warmth and laughter dazzled through the grim reality of poverty and neglect.

Peter Ward, former Head of Norfolk Adoption and Fostering Service

"Respect" is a very important book. It gives voice to the marginalised and dispossessed children who are slipping, in ever greater numbers, through the safety net which a civilised society should provide to protect and support them. It is the moving story of an independent charitable organisation, set up by people who could no longer accept the way the system was failing the most vulnerable. No matter how difficult or challenging these kids were, "Respect" vowed never to give up on any of *them. This book should be compulsory reading for all politicians and be a core text on teacher training courses.*

Martin Phillips, former Local Authority Adviser

When I was at school Dom was that great teacher that you never forget, who then channeled that energy into working with the "hardest to reach" kids at Respect4us. This is a compelling and beautifully written account of working with those children: by turns inspiring, frustrating, funny, hopeful, and desperately sad. But mostly revealing of the lonely world of the most difficult kid in the school. You will look at that child differently after reading this book.

Sandra Weeks, parent, school governor and former student of the author

Contents

Introduction

what the book is about

This is a book about children. None of it is fiction. Most chapters have at their centre, the story of an individual child. It's not the whole story of that child - and possibly not a story that the child herself would recognise - but it is the honest story of how we experienced that child. We know about these children because for ten years we ran an independent alternative education provision in Norfolk called Respect4us.

We have written the book because the work of Respect4us ("R4U" or more frequently just "Respect") was important and needs to be recorded. The focus of the book though is not Respect, nor its staff, but the young people with whom we worked. We always addressed our "clients" as "young people" because as adolescents they didn't like to be thought of as children. However, legally, children are what they were. In this book we refer to them as children because it's important that we, as adults, think of them as children; and that we remember they are worthy of all the protection and care that we should instinctively provide for children.

who should read it

I would like teachers to read it. That's mainly because I'm a teacher and have been one for 45 years. I'll say more about my history in due course - but not too much because this book really is about children. I ought also to acknowledge here that I've switched from first person plural (the authors) to first person singular (just me). The author's voice throughout will be mine but the book is co-authored. Many of the stories are Liz's and she will figure prominently throughout. Liz is not a teacher. Well that's nonsense of course, and by the time you get to the end of the book, I hope you will agree with me that she is one of the most skilled teachers you are ever likely to meet. By "Liz is not

1

a teacher", I mean that she has no professional teaching qualifications. To our partnership I brought the paper qualifications - degree in history, teaching qualification, MA in special education, headteacher qualification, - and she brought the practical teaching skills. I've always done the writing while she has done the talking. I'm the writer of this book but most of the stories are hers.

If you are a teacher, a trainee teacher, a teaching assistant or some other educator, you need to read this book because it is going to tell you about some of the children you will have to work with during your professional life. You may have met some of them already or, if not, I promise you will meet them in whatever sector of education you choose to work. If you work in an alternative provision like R4U or in a "pupil referral unit" or a special school, you are likely to meet very many of them. However, you will also meet them, though in not such large numbers, in any maintained school, primary or secondary, and in tertiary education. You will meet some in the private sector including the grandest of public schools. These pupils will probably be the ones you dread seeing in your class. By reading this book I hope you will lose some of that dread; and I hope you will gain some insight into the lives of the most difficult, challenging, troubled, and damaged children that anyone in education is likely to encounter.

This is not just a book for teachers. It will also be of interest to any of the other professionals whose work brings them into contact with troubled children. Most obviously, youth workers and social workers, and also probation and police officers. I've recently read "Crossing the Line" by John Sutherland, a former Metropolitan Police Chief Superintendent, and I was struck by the extent to which police officers are dealing with these children, or the adults they turn into, and all the problems they cause, every day of their working lives. The average teacher has a comparatively easy job.

This is not just a book for professionals likely to encounter difficult children. Some of the professional skills you will read about are useful for anyone working with young people, not just the most difficult ones; and they are useful skills for any parent to have in their toolkit. I hope it has wider interest for anyone wanting to understand the reasons for educational under-achievement, and the nature of inequality in our society.

about the authors

I began my teacher training in Bristol in 1975 by doing an observation in a large comprehensive school. The teacher I worked with was a skilled practitioner, the head of the history department. The school culture brooked no disruption by pupils and, generally, ill-disciplined pupils were sent out of the classroom. I was young and naive but my experience of this classroom tended to make me feel on the side of the young people. I witnessed a fifteen year old girl get slung out of her history class, lesson after lesson, and feeling a little sorry for her, I suggested to the teacher that I went out and did some individual work with her. The slightly bemused teacher clearly thought I was wasting my time but agreed to let me go, - though with a look on his face that said, "You'll learn soon enough, Sonny."

For my remaining weeks attached to that class, I sat with the girl in the corridor, or we found an empty classroom, and we talked. No..... she talked, I listened, and I learned. She told me about her home life, about her friends, about what she did out of school, about her likes and dislikes, her fears, her hopes and dreams. She honestly couldn't see the point of school and had no time at all for the teachers who from her viewpoint treated her with no respect at all. I learned a huge amount about how a disaffected young person viewed school and what made her tick. I was a trainee and I still had everything to learn about my craft but I took away a lesson from that early experience that has stayed with me throughout my career.

For children from happy, caring, supportive families, school is a wondrous place that can set them free, where they can learn, explore and stretch their wings. But for some children from more disadvantaged backgrounds, school is a quite different

3

experience. Held back as they are, weighed down by pressures, worries, fears and traumas ("adverse childhood experiences" in the jargon) of which they are barely consciously aware, school is a pointless distraction with little relevance to their lives. Of course, as teachers we believe passionately that education is the best route out of squalor, poverty, and human misery. However, if we are ever to convince one of these children that school is important, we need to have the sort of relationship with him or her that a good parent has with their own privileged child - the sort of child who enters school and never looks back.

When I completed my time at that school in Bristol, the girl I'd worked with handed me a letter in which she wished me luck and said that I was going to be a good teacher because I was the only one who had ever listened to her. I carried that letter in my wallet for many years.

The joy of working in an all-ability school is the variety of the work. In one classroom I could be teaching A level history and working with very bright eighteen year olds, a bell goes, and I am on my way to a class of eleven year olds including some with learning or emotional and behavioural difficulties. I loved all of it. Some relationships were easy - I count among my friends, students from my first A level class, now themselves retired and grandparents.

Moving to a school in inner London in the 1980s, I found few classes that were not challenging and, in that school, I learned my craft. I began to realise that though I loved teaching the range of abilities and ages, I was most interested in working with the students no one else seemed to want to teach. There were many teachers who could teach bright and enthusiastic learners but comparatively few who wanted to work with the troubled and disaffected. I took an MA in special educational needs (SEN) and in the 1990s was responsible for the management of SEN at a struggling school in Norfolk. It was in this role that I met Liz.

Liz and I are chalk and cheese. While my upbringing was staid, conventional and middle class, her's was chaotic. Her father was in the air force and she trailed around the World ending her secondary education at school in Norwich where she was not entered for qualifications as her academic records had not followed her. A range of jobs followed: she worked as a window dresser, did office work, organised shows and displays for a newspaper, raised children while shelf stacking and cleaning, and worked in a hospital. Finally, when she applied to me for a job as a learning support assistant, she found her forte.

The job Liz got was to support all the students in our Year 9 (aged 13-14) who were at risk of exclusion. There were many of them. The brief I gave her was to form relationships, become trusted, understand what made these young people tick and to think about how she could move them forward. From the start she was brilliant! She was naturally on the wavelength of the children she worked with. And they adored her. She was so successful that before long the teachers were accepting her judgement about the best approach to take with different youngsters. When she came across a teacher determined to be unco-operative she would, on her own initiative, withdraw children from the classroom before trouble boiled over. She grew in confidence.

At the end of her first school year I decided that Liz should move forward with her year group into Year 10. Within days of the new year starting, she had grasped that there was little to interest and engage her young people in the academic GCSE courses on offer and she began to research what alternatives might be available. She formed an alliance with a police officer responsible for educational liaison, who was working with the school to steer young people away from criminal behaviour, and together they created an activity based programme - which, in time, received certification from the Prince's Trust. Before long her students were involved in community projects involving a massive range of practical and social skills. The young people were winning awards. Liz was winning awards, being congratulated by Prince Charles himself, and being invited to a Buckingham Palace garden party.

5

Liz's secret lay in knowing how to make school fun and interesting for these young people. She made them want to get up in the morning and turn up to school every day. She listened and dealt with all the problems and pain life was throwing at them. She got to know their families, their social workers, their dreams and aspirations. She gave them love and they recognised it; because they trusted her, they took the tough talking she often gave them; they knew she was always fighting their corner. She never gave up on them.

A feature of Liz's work was the use of residential experiences and she built into her course as many of these as she could. Staying away from home, culture and normal society is quite the most transformative experience young people from disadvantaged backgrounds can be given..

I achieved one of my own professional peaks when I stood at the top of Snowdon with a child, who had whined, grizzled and protested all the way up; at that moment I knew, from the look on her face, that she was appreciating, for the first time ever, the wonder and majesty of a mountain-top view, experiencing those awesome 'top of the world' and 'close to heaven' feelings; and I knew this might never happen to her again but that she would always remember it.

I saw pride in young faces as they achieved each of the physical or mental challenges thrown at them - getting to the top of a rock face, emerging gasping for breath from a sump when caving, wriggling from a kayak, soaked and exhausted at the bottom of a set of rapids, going over the parapet of a viaduct and abseiling into a void. Most important of all was the camaraderie, the knowledge, the understanding and the trust that developed within each group and between the young people and their leaders over the course of a week-long residential. It underlined for me just how limited is the normal school experience, constrained by a regimented curriculum, a fixed school routine and a very short day. During a week away the ability of a teacher to influence the life of a young person is increased by multiples.

We would return to normal school life with a hugely increased awareness and understanding of who these children were, the problems they faced, and what they were capable of achieving. In the school context they remained very challenging young people and the battles to protect them were constant. They still had to attend lessons in core subjects and the chances of achieving success with an unsympathetic teacher were very limited. Flare-ups and aggressive confrontations were regular. The frequent changes of leadership, not uncommon in a small and struggling school, made life more difficult and at times the continuation of our work looked precarious.

It was on residential trips that Liz and I began to talk about how we could transform these children's lives, if we were free to give them the education we knew they needed, if we were free to motivate them and inspire them in the ways that we knew worked. Most of them had already given up on school and its ability to give them anything they wanted or needed. We faced a constant struggle to keep them in school; it was a regular fight against the cynicism of colleagues who had written off these young people; it was a battle to persuade our youngsters to keep trying, and to convince them that school still had something to offer them. In reality their lives were often so chaotic that a completely different approach was needed. On a daily basis these children faced issues and pressures that few of us could imagine coping with. It really shouldn't be a surprise to anyone that they mess up so often in school.

Again and again our conversation would come back to how we might create the space and freedom to do this work full-time as our own bosses. Respect4us was the result.

about the company

Our company, Respect4us Community Interest Company was an independent alternative educational provision. It opened its doors in 2010 and was wound up at the end of 2019. Over the decade it worked with several thousand children from across Norfolk. There are a number of alternative providers in Norfolk offering non-academic, vocational routes for young people as an alternative or supplement to traditional schooling. Respect was different from the others in that it specialised in behaviour. Its expertise in working with the most challenging children in the County came to be widely recognised. On behalf of Respect4us, I was honoured in the 2020 New Year's Honours List with an MBE for services to alternative education in Norfolk.

Respect4us was not a school so most of the regulations governing schools did not apply. For example there was no requirement to teach the National Curriculum. All children who came to Respect were on the roll of a school and they remained the responsibility of that school. So schools had to satisfy themselves that the children were safe and that Respect was meeting their needs. No child came to us for the whole week and all continued to receive some academic education at their home school. The school, not Respect4us, was accountable to Ofsted for the children's education. This removed from us much of the pressure schools experience and gave us considerable freedom to design a curriculum tailored to the individual needs of our children.

We operated from a unit on an industrial estate in Norwich, well away from any school. We took children from all over Norfolk delivered by taxi or collected in one of our minibuses. This unit remained the centre of all operations but in time we opened satellite units in Great Yarmouth and in Swaffham, and a unit for primary aged children near Coltishall.

What made us successful was the quality of our staff and they were rarely professional teachers. During the course of the book I will explore what made many of these individuals outstanding at what they did and will return to it again in the conclusion.

This book is primarily about children and not a lot of attention will be paid to the mechanics and operations of the organisation though I will address some aspects where they are relevant to

8

how we dealt with children. I will return to these in the conclusion and address the reasons why the work of Respect4us came to an end in 2019.

Each of the children who attended Respect4us had a unique story. We have selected just a few to tell you about. We tell their stories as we saw them. We knew very little about any of their lives before they came to us other than what they themselves told us. Occasionally we would be given a few details by the school, especially when there were safeguarding issues of which they needed us to be aware. Normally we didn't ask too many questions, preferring to take the children as we found them and to have as few preconceptions as possible. We wanted the children to have an opportunity to re-create themselves when they came to us. We wanted them to know that whatever had happened in their past, we had not prejudged them. We were concerned only about their futures.

Having read a chapter about an individual, you may want to know what happened to them ultimately. Unfortunately there is no R4U alumni club where old students meet to talk about the good old days and where they can share the triumphs and disasters of their lives. This makes assessing our long term success difficult, but in the short term at least, we know we turned most of these children around. From time to time we did get information about how our students had prospered after leaving us and I will include details where I can.

All the children's names are fictitious and some details have been changed to preserve their anonymity. Throughout the decade a daily diary was kept recording in detail everything that happened that day. When the company was wound up these diaries were destroyed for data protection reasons (this broke my heart as an historian); so the stories in this book are based on the collective memory of the staff. None of it is fiction but in the interests of storytelling sometimes the order of events are changed and separate stories amalgamated. Much of the

9

dialogue is invented but is true to the real conversations we actually had.

1 Rec Up
how we worked

Let me start by telling you a little more about how we worked, and the importance we put on relationships and understanding our young people. This story opens when we had been operating for just a few months.

I was standing in the middle of the workshop, looking around. It seemed noisy, chaotic even. There were teenagers in all directions. I quickly reassured myself that there was perhaps some order and purpose to it. To one side of the workshop, Jason was attempting to teach bricklaying while his students seemed more interested in flicking mortar at each other with their trowels. On the other side, the group led by Donna had probably put more paint on their overalls, hands and faces than on the bird boxes which they'd made the previous day and which they were now supposed to be painting.

I had entered the workshop with Ricky to have another look at the large open canoe with a hole in the bottom that he had spotted on ebay and which he and I had collected only that morning. I had promised we would make a decision about whether we were going to repair it but only after he had completed his literacy work and done some reading with me. Keeping Ricky focused had been exhausting, for me at least. Now the drudgery was over he was bursting with energy, talking excitedly about how he would fix the canoe. He was itching to get on with it but I was reluctant to give the go-ahead. Rather than Ricky's suspect judgement, I wanted Jason's expert opinion, but could see he was busy.

The canoe was on trestles and Ricky, getting bored, climbed inside with his legs through the hole. Now showing off, he was calling to his mates to look at him. The bricklayers were instantly distracted and began to drift over, to Jason's obvious frustration and irritation.

11

Just as I was about to intervene, a hush fell, first over the bird boxers and then among the bricklayers; everyone stopped in their tracks. When even Ricky fell silent, I knew something was up. I turned to look around.

Standing in the open, sunlit, garage doorway, were two dark figures with silhouettes that suggested they might be police officers. The silence seemed to deepen. I stared, squinting into the sun; and then, trying to see more clearly, I moved towards the figures in the bright doorway. As I did so, I was aware of a sudden flurry of movement to each side, and behind me.

"Hello," I said, as I approached the two figures. Yes, they were police officers.
"I'm Dom. What can I do for you?"

Getting closer, I realised the officers were looking, not at me, but at what was going on over my shoulder. I turned in the direction they were staring and saw most of the young people piling out in panic through the fire exit at the back of the workshop. Ricky was struggling to extricate himself from the hole in the boat. Reassuringly, I noticed Donna and Jason already moving to deal with whatever was going to happen out behind the unit.

I turned back to face the officers. Now close up, I could see these were women police officers. No, I thought, not police officers but police community support officers, PCSOs; and very young-looking.

"Hello," I said again.
"What happened?" one of them asked, nodding towards the fire door now swinging ajar.
"Oh, break time," I replied, casually.
"I'm Dom," I continued. "I'm in charge here …. or," smiling, "that's what I like to think. What brings you round? Social visit or business?"
"Sorry! I'm Jenny …"
"…and I'm Laura."

"We patrol the neighbourhood and the estate. Just popping in to introduce ourselves," said Jenny.

"We recognise some of your..er...clients," said Laura, "from the neighbourhood."

"So, what do you do here?" asked Jenny.

"We're an independent alternative education provision," I replied.

"What's that mean?"

"It means we look after the kids who are in trouble. Kids mostly excluded from mainstream schools. We work closely with the pupil referral units which are responsible for excluded children, and we have many who are on their roll. Some mainstream schools send us youngsters who are in danger of being excluded - they recognise they need help in turning them around. That's what we're expert at."

"So you take all the bad ones .... from just round here or across the City?" said Laura.

"We take from across the County not just the City. And I prefer 'troubled' to 'bad'. Many of them have unimaginably horrible lives - though I guess you must know that - and it should be no surprise they can't cope with school. Most are here for behavioural reasons but not all of them. Some are just oddballs. Some are victims of bullying in school. Some are school refusers. We get the occasional pregnant girl. A surprising number are on the autistic spectrum and schools can't cope with them."

"Interesting," said Jenny. "So what's going on in here?" she said, nodding towards the workshop. "What were they all doing when we arrived?"

"A number of things. There's woodwork.....they made the bird boxes over there. Now they're decorating them. Bricklaying over here. These are all projects that they have suggested, things they wanted to learn to do. Maybe for one or two, it will plant an idea for a trade and they'll go on to develop it at college, but for most it's just a life skill.......they'll be better at DIY. But that's not the point......all the time, we are working, without them realising it, on the vital social skills - communication, co-operation, working together, following instructions, organisation, self-discipline, completing a task, experiencing achievement etc etc."

13

"Aren't they supposed to be doing National Curriculum?" asked Laura.

"In theory…..yes, because they are school age. But the reality for most is no education at all. Schools, in some cases, have washed their hands of them. We are definitely not a school. We're an AP, an alternative provision. Our job is to turn these kids around if at all possible. We listen to them in a way many schools these days seem unable to do. We then design a curriculum that meets their individual needs. We have to be very flexible for it to work. We have to engage them. So a lot of the time it will appear that we are simply entertaining them. But that's how we reach them. For us to make any progress, they have to decide that they want to come to us. Above all, this has to be a place they feel safe, where they feel respected, where they feel wanted …. and loved."

"So you don't do any academic work like in school?" persisted Laura.

"That's not what I said," I responded. "It's not our prime focus but we do some book work. We start every day with half an hour of literacy and numeracy. They each have an individual programme which they can start as soon as they arrive in the morning. Nothing else happens until that is completed. Then we talk about the rest of the day and we all agree what we are going to do. It can take a long time, but it is important that they feel they have some say. Again, they are practising those social skills I mentioned. Some may end up doing more reading, writing or maths if that's part of their programme. Many of them have shockingly low levels of literacy, and they know that, and they decide to do something about it. It happens especially with the older ones when we start doing college applications. Often we will leave the older ones behind to get on with that - supervised of course - while the younger ones go out for physical activity."

"So are you all teachers?" asked Jenny

"I am a qualified teacher but most of the staff here are not. They have jobs here because they are absolutely brilliant at engaging with troubled young people."

"Interesting," she said.

"You said you'd recognised some of our young people. How's that?" I asked.

"Well, we've been having a crackdown on the youngsters who gather in the evenings down in the park. There's a lot of them down there at the moment. We know there's always alcohol and now there's known dealers mixing in with them. In street talk it's called a 'rec up'"

"That means a meet-up at the recreation ground," interrupted Laura. "We break them up, take their names and addresses, and send them home with a warning. Sometimes we nab a drug dealer, caught in possession."

"Well, we don't do it," said Jenny. "We don't have the powers. We're PCSOs. It's our colleagues who do all that stuff. We observe, remember names and faces, and then we follow up. Maybe make a home visit, meet the parents, find out more about the kids and what's going for them. Around here we are the eyes and ears of the Force. We need to know what's going on, on the ground."

"Now that sounds like sensible community policing," I said. "Got time for a coffee?"

We got to hear a lot about 'rec ups' in the following weeks and months. The PCSOs would call in most Fridays to join us for a coffee. Gradually the young people got used to having the officers around and didn't all run out of the fire door when they arrived. The officers were both attractive and personable young women and the older boys in particular took to joining in at the kitchen table and chatting flirtatiously with them. It was rare for young people immersed in street culture to have an opportunity to meet and get to know police officers as human beings outside conflict situations. We were proud of being able to facilitate the education of both sides. The officers were able to start seeing the youngsters differently as they learned about their troubled lives - although of course we did realise they were really there to gather intelligence.

When now the police arrived in one of the parks to break up a 'rec up', these two could defuse conflict easily by being able to reel off the names of many present and simply telling them to 'hop it'. Familiar and friendly relations had many benefits for the community. When there was trouble on the estate, maybe vandalism or anti-social behaviour, the police could often identify the culprits from the victim's description and the problem could be terminated by a simple quiet word. There were real benefits to the youngsters from having the police on their side; a quiet ticking off was a lot better all-round than an arrest and a court appearance; and then there were the times the kids found themselves with a broken bike and a PCSO would come to the rescue; or the times when they had been drinking too much or were completely out of it on other substances and the police got them home. So much conflict is down to human relationships and is so easily side-stepped with a little mutual effort to understand one another.

We were great believers in good community policing and we loved our PCSOs. This type of officer had not been around for long. They were introduced in the early 2000s and had a role similar to that of the teaching assistant in schools. Their value to Respect was that they had the time to drop in and get to know the youngsters, unlike warranted officers who arrived in police cars only when there was trouble. This softer approach paid dividends as we were well aware that our young people were responsible for much of the anti-social behaviour in the community. We felt this was community policing that really worked. Unfortunately in 2018 the County abolished the role of PCSO, the only force in the country to do so. They didn't consult us about it.

2 Shaun

troubled families

I don't want to get into the contentious debate that has been going on for centuries about the existence of an "under-class"; however, our current society clearly has a problem with a considerable number of families with multiple problems that are intergenerational. It was recognised in 2011 when David Cameron launched the Troubled Families Programme aiming to turn around some 120,000 troubled families (later extended to 400,000). He said these families were:

"the source of a large proportion of the problems in society: drug addiction, alcohol abuse, crime, a culture of disruption and irresponsibility that cascades down the generations". [1]

He promised that by 2015 the programme would have got children back into school, have reduced crime and anti-social behaviour, got adults on the path back into work, and reduced the costs of these families to the public sector (£9 billion according to the Prime Minister).

In May 2015 the Department for Communities and Local Government proudly announced that the programme had been successful in turning around 99% of troubled families. However, in October 2016 the National Institute for Economic and Social Research was finally allowed to publish its finding that the programme had had *"no significant or systemic impact on outcomes related to employment, job seeking, school attendance, or anti-social behaviour."* [2]

Our local experience at Respect4us, admittedly on a very small scale, would seem to confirm the finding of the NIESR. Turning families around is not a simple matter that can be achieved in a few years.

---

[1] Speech by David Cameron on plans to improve services for troubled families. Published 15 Dec 2011.

[2] "National Evaluation of the Troubled Families Programme". Institute of Economic and Social Research Oct 2016.

Shaun's case illustrates some aspects of what we were up against. The story starts as Jason and I set off to find this 15 year old who had not been in school for a very long time.

The crescent seemed to go on forever. Few of the houses were numbered, which made finding the one we were looking for difficult. Our minibus was now deep inside a sprawling housing estate of small semi-detached or terraced houses; an estate that came from an age when public housing was built on a massive scale; a maze, with streets so alike we felt completely lost. This crescent was one of the bleakest examples of its streets.

Many of what could have once been front gardens were now scrapyards containing wheel-less cars, with axles supported by bricks, and piles of no longer wanted white goods - rusting fridges, cookers and washing machines. Every so often we would pass a garden with fences intact, a mown patch of grass and well-kept flower borders and shrubs, but there were very few of these. When we eventually found Shaun's place it was only identifiable because the house to the left of it was well-maintained and its front door had a number. We had by now worked out which way the numbers ran so we knew this had to be the one.

Jason pulled up to the kerb, switched off the engine and turned to me. The two teenage boys in the back of the bus had seemed nervous about coming here to find Shaun, and had tried to dissuade us.
"I dunno why you're bothered," said one of them. "I've known Shaun for years. He ain't coming."
"You came out this morning," I said. "When you heard what we had planned, you agreed to give it a try. Maybe Shaun will be the same."
"You don't know Shaun," said the same boy.
"We have to give him the chance to say 'No', lads," said Jason.
We looked at each other again.
"You or me?" said Jason.

"Shall we both go? I feel like I need moral support, if not protection. You're younger and fitter than I am," I said, smiling nervously.

Jason shrugged. "Yeh, right!" he said. "Come on, I'll look after you."

Simultaneously, we opened the front doors of the bus and stepped down. Having slammed his door shut, Jason thought again, re-opened it, reached in, and removed the keys from the ignition. "Safety first, eh?" he said as he joined me on the pavement.

Jason had been with us from the start. Liz and I had got to know him as a Technology assistant and cover supervisor at our school and he had been our first recruit when we broke out to form our own company. He had skills that proved invaluable. He was a builder, carpenter, plumber, artist, craftsman, sportsman and was knowledgeable about history, art and science. He built walls, taught brick-laying, fitted our kitchen, mended bikes, did our plumbing, put up display boards, designed, carved and painted our exterior logos, mended our wrecked minibuses, gave art classes, took children on day-trips to London to visit art galleries, played football and was just brilliant at talking to young people. We would never have managed in those early days without Jason.

I was in the street with him one day, when we saw a couple of our kids being threatened by a group of young male adults; Jason waded straight in, fearless in his defence of our youngsters, and sent the group packing. After that I always felt safe when I was out and about with him. He was a kind, gentle, lovely man, but tough with a streetfighter's edge to him. Our youngsters loved him. He was an amazing colleague who would go anywhere and be up for anything and everything. He personified the qualities that make working with difficult teenagers look easy.

So, with Jason beside me, I felt quite safe as we contemplated the wreck of a house in front of us. The ground floor front window was smashed and a board had been propped behind it.

The front door was ajar but there really wasn't a lot left of it. It appeared to have been staved in on the side around the lock with splinters of bare wood showing. The top hinge was hanging loose on its screws, and what remained of the door looked as though it could fall out at any moment. The floor under the door was littered with unopened, trampled mail.

Jason leaned forward and knocked on the door frame, calling softly, "Hello."

There was silence.

"I'm not going in," I whispered.

"Shall we leave it?" asked Jason.

"No, I can't go back and face Liz unless we've really tried our best."

I looked round to check the bus. The two boys were studiously gazing out of the opposite window, establishing that what we were doing was nothing at all to do with them.

Turning back to the open door I yelled, "Mrs Carter."

After a moment there was a noise above our heads. A window opened.

"Whadya want?"

The face above belonged to a middle aged woman who appeared to be wearing a dressing gown.

"Mrs Carter?"

"Maybe."

"We've come for Shaun. We're from a company called Respect4us. His school has asked us to pick him up. They wrote to you about it. He's going to work with us now."

"Nah, Shaun don't do school. Dunno about no letter."

"Well we're not school. We're an alternative provision. We think Shaun should try it. He might enjoy it."

We became aware that the door had swung more ajar and a youth with a scowl on his face was studying us. He was tall and gangly, and wearing only a T-shirt and boxers.

"What?" he said, aggressively.

"Are you Shaun?" I asked.

"What do you want?"

"I'm Dom and this is Jason. We're alternative education…. called Respect4us. We're here to help… don't worry … we're not here to give you grief. Maybe get you into college next year or help you find a job. Look, ... we are definitely not taking you back to school."

"I'm done with all that."

"I know," I said.

Jason stepped forward. "I've got a 'Goals' pitch booked for this afternoon. Fancy a game of five-a-side? We've got Gavin and Stuart in the bus. They're mates of yours, aren't they? They've agreed to play."

"I'm not dressed. And I'm hungry."

"We can wait until you've got some clothes on. And we can do some breakfast back at the unit. It's not far. Do you eat bacon rolls?"

"We'll wait for you in the bus. Five minutes?"

We both turned and walked away. Shaun stood for a moment looking at us, looking at the bus and the two shady figures inside, then turned inside. Two minutes later he was back wearing tracksuit bottoms and hopping as he pulled on a pair of trainers. He ran across to the open side door of the minibus and climbed in. I slid the side door shut and then climbed into the front passenger seat alongside Jason.

I leaned round with my arm over the back of the seat. Shaun was sitting a row back. The other two boys were in the back seats. So far they had said nothing to each other.

Jason watched in his rear-view mirror.

"Lads, you all need to put your seat belts on."

Nobody moved.

"Shaun, can you put your belt on. Please," I said, looking at him and getting eye contact.

"Jason isn't allowed to move the bus until we are all belted. We want to get back as quick as we can so we can all get something to eat."

"Yeh, if we don't hurry the gannets back there will have had all the bacon," added Jason, helpfully.

After a moment's more hesitation, Shaun reached for the belt, pulled it across his chest and fastened it.

The two boys at the back then fastened their belts.

Jason started up and pulled away from the kerb.

"So what position do you play Shaun?" he said. "I bet you're usually defence aren't you? But you could also be a handy striker. You know you're built like Peter Crouch?"

"Whaat?.....faaaack off!"

"What do you two in the back think? Shaun any good?"

"S'okay," muttered Gavin, looking vacantly out of the side window.

"Would you want him on your team, Gav?" asked Jason.

"No," interrupted Shaun, "Would I have HIM on MY team?" He then answered his own question, "I don't think so!"

Stuart laughed.

"Whatever," said Gavin, still staring into the distance.

We drove in silence for a few moments.

"So what happened to your front door Shaun? It's a bit of a mess," I said.

"Police came.... For my brother."

"What? For Terry?" asked Stuart.

"It took an army of them. They had helmets and masks and some of them had guns. They could have just knocked on the door, but no, they had to smash it in."

"Was this last night?" I asked.

"Nah, early morning, yesterday."

"Where's your brother now?"

"Dunno"

"Is your mum ok?"

"My mum? How would I know?"

"Was that your mum we just saw?"

"That was my nan."

"Your nan? Was she upset?"

"She can't stand Terry. She said, 'Good riddance!' and said they were welcome to him. She said she didn't even know he was there. He must have come in during the night to sleep on the settee."

"What's he done?"

"Nothing. They're all just bastards. They don't like none of my brothers....... Anyway, you ask a lot of questions, you do."

Jason turned on Radio 1. There was no more conversation.

22

Quite a lot of the morning was spent making breakfast. Shaun seemed a little shocked that he had to make his own bread. Donna had brought in an old bread maker that she no longer used at home and I'd started off a load of dough earlier that morning. Shaun couldn't believe that he would be eating this. He wouldn't do it himself but he watched as I cut the dough into roll portions and set them aside to prove. While this happened he went into the next room to play pool with Stuart. When the game was over he returned to the kitchen. He was clearly hungry and wanted to eat. I explained that the rolls now had to bake in the oven.

"It'll only take ten minutes."

"What's the point, man? You can just buy them in the shop around the corner."

"These will be better. Let's cook the bacon while we're waiting."

"Nah. I'll play more pool."

Shaun could not be persuaded to take part in any of the cooking but kept coming back to observe what I was doing. When he was finally handed his hot bacon roll on a plate, he looked at it suspiciously. He took it away with him into the next room where another game of pool was underway. A few moments later I heard him say, "Man, this is well lush!"

Almost instantly the kitchen filled with boys from the pool room all demanding bacon rolls.

Shaun played football that afternoon and remained on our books for the rest of the year. His attendance was very erratic and sometimes he would disappear during the day if he didn't like what we were doing or had somewhere better to be. He was probably the most hopeless case of all the young people we worked with that year. He really was too far gone but we liked to think we had pulled him back just a little - socialised him slightly, perhaps helped him to trust authority a tiny bit.

Shaun lived entirely in the present with little regard for the consequences of his actions, so we talked to him a lot about his future options and the life he wanted to have. As far as he ever gave any thought to the future, he was fatalistic, "What's the point, man?" He was used to the immediate gratification of his wants, and the idea of sacrificing a pleasure today for the sake of some goal for tomorrow was completely alien to him. If bad consequences followed, well, that was just how life was. There was little sign that we had any impact but we kept at it; using every opportunity to plant the idea that it was possible to make good things happen for yourself in the future by a little thought, planning and work today. We liked to think that this work had some effect, and had planted some idea in his head that paid off eventually. But we had no evidence.

Practically, we made sure he had a CV, had completed a college application and done interview practice. We tried our very best to make sure he had some education in drugs, health and relationships.

Did he get to college? Probably not.
Did he get to prison? Probably.

Needless to say, we saw nothing of the £1.3 billion Cameron's Government spent on the Troubled Families Programme.

3 Ricky
the trouble with schools

It might seem obvious but it needs to be said. Our education system is the result of politics. Our politicians make political choices about how schools should be organised and operated. Nowadays, teachers have little say in what children learn or how they should learn it and be assessed on it. We have a very centralised and tightly controlled education system. It was to escape that system that we set up Respect4us.

Our education system works for most children but not all of them. There are some children who have huge difficulty being in a classroom and schools find it very difficult to adapt and accommodate them. Ricky was one of these. His story starts before Respect had even opened its doors for business.

It was the end of August, the week before term started and I was sitting in a school reception area waiting for yet another appointment with a headteacher. All summer I had been trawling round the high schools trying to drum up business. I was worried. I was still unsure whether our new business was viable. We had our premises but would we have any paying customers?

A woman entered reception with a youth trailing after her. They sat down. I looked at the young man a second time.
"Excuse me, you look very familiar. Have we met?" I asked.
"Hello, Mr Boddington," the youth responded.
"Umm...... how do I know you?"
"I'm Ricky. I was at your school... in Year 8. I helped you film the school concert. Remember?"
"Ricky...? Weren't you...? Didn't you...?" I began, awkwardly.
"Yes," interrupted the woman. "He was in hospital... after the accident... for more than a year. After that I wanted him to go to a different school, so he started here in Year 10."
"You're....?"
"Yeh, his mum."

"Mrs..?"

"Graham. Mrs Graham."

"Hello, Mrs Graham. I don't think I remember meeting you when Ricky was with us. So Ricky missed .... What? ... a year and a half of school? That must have been difficult to catch up."

"I thought a fresh start would help," she paused, "he was excited to come back to school but it didn't last."

"So are you waiting to see the Head?" I smiled, "in trouble like me?"

"Yes, he got sent home too many times last year. None of the teachers wanted him in their classes. He's been out of school for ages now so we are here to see what's going to happen to him in Year 11."

At that point the secretary told me to go through to see the headteacher.

"Good luck," I said to Ricky and his mum, as I steeled myself to open the forbidding door labelled 'HEAD'.

This was a headteacher for whom I had a lot of respect. She ran a school that was now a struggling comprehensive. Yet, in its heyday in the 1970s, it was large - 1200 pupils - and catered for all abilities. At that time it was superbly equipped with workshops for all types of trade, a hair-dressing salon, kitchens, even a flat where young people could learn and practice almost every type of practical life skill from cooking and cleaning to dress making, putting up shelves and baby care. Some young people left school with little in the way of academic qualifications but they were ready for life; they'd had good careers advice from a very active local authority careers service; they had jobs and apprenticeships lined up; they were well equipped with practical, life and social skills; they had emotional resilience, purpose in life and could envisage their futures. The beauty of the comprehensive school was that decisions about the route you were taking through life could be put off until later - no 'sheep and goats' division at age 11. There was plenty there in the school for older children who had had enough of academic education. Choices could be made as you moved through the school but they didn't have to be permanent. The great majority of young people followed the traditional academic route, and like many comprehensives this school had a healthily large sixth form, each year sending many students to university, including some to Oxford and Cambridge.

Comprehensive education meant secondary schools catered for all children, whatever their needs, interests and abilities. The idea of comprehensive education was idealistic but not, in my opinion, unreasonably so. Would we have today's inequality and divisions in our society if we had persisted with the idea? It was in 1965 that the Government required Local Authorities to submit plans for comprehensivisation but almost immediately it became a political football that was kicked to and fro through the 1970s. Then two developments of the 1980s killed off comprehensive education. First, all the imaginative ways in which young people had been engaged in their own learning were swept away by the National Curriculum introduced in 1988, so that now, by law, all children followed the same academic "grammar school" curriculum.

The second development was that parents were allowed to decide which school their children should attend and there were no longer catchment areas. The policy was called 'parental choice' but the practical effect was actually to limit choice. The more aspirational parents fought to get their children into the schools in the area thought to be better and other schools ended up with more than their fair share of troubled children. The process was self-perpetuating. Many parents prefer their children not to be mixing with the "rougher" sorts of kids. It's completely understandable but is it good for society?

This headteacher presided over a school that had been in slow decline over the previous two decades. There were half the number of pupils there had once been, and these tended to be from the less aspirational families. To put it bluntly, the school's children were from families who were poor, often single parents, usually of low educational attainment themselves, and for these families life was a continual uphill struggle. The pressure on heads and teachers in schools like this is relentless. Unless they can show steady improvement in exam results the school

27

continues its slide towards the abyss. Ofsted inspections become more frequent. The school is given an even wider berth by more aspirational families. It becomes harder to recruit good teachers. As the pressure increases it becomes more and more difficult to provide in school what some children need most. Everyone wants the best for children but sometimes what children need most is not an improved academic grade.

The temptation for school leaders is simply to remove the children who don't fit - to 'exclude' (a legal process that can be challenged), or to suggest to parents that they might like to find another school before the child does get excluded. Some children stop attending and just get quietly 'off-rolled'. Coupled with 'zero-tolerance' policies, or 'three strikes and you're out', these sorts of measures have turned around challenging schools up and down the country while exclusion rates have soared.. However, the headteacher I was about to meet was not one of those who went for the easy solutions. She fought for every single one of her children.

When she agreed to see me, I don't know exactly what she was expecting but almost immediately we found ourselves talking about Ricky. Within twenty minutes I was pretty certain I had a customer! The Head asked Mrs Graham if she minded me staying on for their meeting and she agreed. We reached agreement very quickly that Ricky would be attending Respect4us, and would only have to go into school for his core lessons.

Ricky was delighted and was my new best friend. He was so keen he wanted to go and see our premises straightaway. With mum's agreement he came back to the unit with me for a look around. We had only recently taken over an industrial unit and were hard at work getting it ready for the start of term. I was particularly happy to show our setup to Ricky because I wanted to see it through the eyes of a young person who would be a consumer of what we were creating.

At the heart of the unit was a kitchen with a table that could seat about twelve, and a few more if we all squeezed up. There were all the facilities and equipment that one would expect to find in a large, modern domestic kitchen. We intended to do a lot of cooking and have as many sit down communal meals as possible. This was to be at the centre of our "family" life.

To one side of the kitchen was a large workshop. It had a roll-up door giving access to the apron at the front of the unit, and allowing vehicles to be driven in. We envisaged it as a multi-purpose space for art and craft work, woodwork, engineering and mechanical projects, and for tinkering with cars and bikes. We had a pool table that was used here and table tennis. There was a lot of storage space. Beyond the workshop was our office and visitor reception.

To the other side of the kitchen was our classroom, equipped with chairs, tables, desktop computers and display boards. This room had exterior access to the front of the unit. Behind the kitchen and linking to the classroom was a relaxation room with sofas, comfortable chairs and a large wall mounted screen for video games, films and television. A serving hatch allowed visual observation from the kitchen. Leading off the relaxation room was another office space for staff use and individual or very small group counselling work.

Ricky seemed impressed and bubbled over with ideas for improvements. From then on we couldn't get rid of him even though we didn't officially open until the following week. The next morning he was waiting for us to arrive, and then spent that day helping Jason build dividing walls. Over the week he developed plans for a cabled intranet and was then leaping about drilling holes in walls and laying cable all over the building. He had far more knowledge of IT than any of us and before long he had all the ancient donated computers, networked and up and running.

Ricky had a big smile and an infectious enthusiasm that was hard to resist. He would get an idea into his head and straightway start putting it into practice, charging ahead, brushing aside or trampling underfoot any objections. It was very hard to say "No" to Ricky. At least Jason and I found it hard, Liz did it regularly and he didn't like it. We began to realise that he had been spoiled rotten by his mum who had clearly over-compensated for his accident and long convalescence. Being stood up to and thwarted was a new experience and one that he never really got used to.

Despite this flaw there was something irresistible about Ricky. He just needed to be busy, constantly leaping about doing things. He would have been a nightmare in a classroom, but he loved adult company and was desperate to please and be of service. Throughout that first year of Respect4us, Ricky was our 'go-to' person when anything needed doing. So when Jason began teaching bricklaying, it was Ricky who would mix the cement and organise all the materials. It was Ricky who organised the digging up of our Christmas tree and its erection in the workshop - all 20 feet of it! It was Ricky who toured the scrapyards with Jason to find parts for our mechanical scarecrow. This was a project that evolved from our country walks. When scarecrows were pointed out and discussed someone noticed that they did a very poor job of scaring off the birds which led to a detailed discussion about how they might be improved. Someone pointed out that if they waved their arms about they might stand more chance of scaring the crows. Before long Ricky and his fellow engineers had designed and built a robotic scarecrow, with windscreen wiper motors making the arms wave, all driven by a car battery built into the scarecrow's backside. It was very impressive and the plan was to mass produce it and sell it to Norfolk farmers. Unfortunately as Ricky and Jason's tour of the scrapyards revealed, car parts like windscreen wiper motors were valuable and in very short supply.

The same drive that made him want to impress adults also drove him to try to impress peers, and here he was not so successful. He had learned over the years that what seemed to get admiration or at least laughter from his peers was outrageously silly behaviour. He took the most terrible physical risks and it was this that had led to his accident involving high voltage electricity cables earlier in his high school career. Once started he didn't know when to stop. He just didn't know how to be with people of his own age. Anyone slightly younger or impressionistic would get the show-off treatment. Those of his own age viewed him as an idiot and he didn't know how to form normal relationships with them. He was clearly intimidated and frightened by some of the other sixteen year olds.

It began to be apparent to us why Ricky had failed at school. There was his restless energy that meant he could not sit still at a desk. Academically, he had gradually fallen behind his peers and given up trying a long time ago. His literacy was almost non-existent and he had no interest at all in trying to improve it. Then there was his lack of social skills around his peers, his lack of common sense, his irresponsible behaviour and the ease with which he could be led astray. On the plus side he was a genius with his hands, he had great capacity to concentrate and complete difficult practical tasks, he had huge drive and determination and he was a born salesperson and entrepreneur.

It was his final year and we were determined that Ricky should leave school with functional literacy and numeracy. We worked very hard at planting the idea that he would go on from us to college. He played along in his charming way and would even sit down for five minutes to practice reading but it was all a game to keep us happy.

He didn't go to college. His mum shielded him and then he went to work. A year and a half later he had a partner and his own child and he was setting up his own IT business. He's probably a millionaire by now.

4 Simon

emotional neglect

I will return more than once to the issue of troubled families. This chapter is about the inability of some families to provide the security, the consistency, the care and especially the love that all children need. This has devastating consequences for the lives of those children and not least, on their ability to thrive at school.

We discovered that Ricky had a brother. It was a surprise because we knew Ricky lived at home on his own with his mum. He had been telling us for some time that his brother was going to come to us, and as we'd heard no more we thought this was probably some fantasy of his. One day we had a number of boys starting with us from the Pupil Referral Unit. One of them was a very tall, very broad and very blond boy called Simon. He and Ricky greeted each other like long-lost brothers, which of course is what they were. When they attended on the same days together they would engage in loud, and generally foul, laddish conversation of which we rapidly began to weary.

The solution was, as far as possible, to have them on different days and when clashes were unavoidable, to make sure that Ricky was engaged separately in Year 11 activities focused on preparation for college. The younger ones would often be taken out for country walks which was never a popular activity - it seldom is for teenagers. I used to motivate them by inventing games and things to do along the way, otherwise the whining became unbearable. On one particular occasion when Simon was present and we were walking through a pine forest, I suggested we had a competition to see who could throw a pine cone the furthest. Liz and a group of girls were walking fifty yards or so ahead and I suggested we throw in their direction to see who could get the closest to them. Simon, as I said, was a big strong lad, with a much more powerful throw than me and he hit Liz squarely in the back with a pine cone. She was wearing a heavy coat, no harm done, but nonetheless distinctly unamused, so I had to step in, apologise and take the blame. However, the boys were now keen on this game, and as long as they didn't aim at the girls I let the throwing continue. They were soon darting in and out of the trees chucking cones at each other - and at me, and to be fair I was throwing a few back. I had just thrown a cone and hit Simon when I realised the girls were way ahead of us. I told the boys we had to catch up and set off up the path. Then my world went black momentarily and I found myself nose down on the path. Simon had thrown not a cone but a log which had struck me on the back of the neck. The boys thought this was very funny. Simon didn't know whether to laugh or be upset but he did help me up. Of course I pointed out to him that there was a world of difference between throwing a pine cone weighing a few grams and a log weighing a couple of kilos, but really I had only myself to blame. This was certainly the opinion of Liz who had no sympathy for me at all as I nursed my bruised head and ego for the rest of the day. Even at my age I needed to be reminded not to play with fire.

Simon continually used the foulest language and could be incredibly rude, defiant and unpleasant but bit by bit we began to discover the kind and thoughtful boy who was hidden inside the ugly shell. As incident after incident was played out, he began to learn that we never gave up on him, that he could perhaps trust us, that he could reveal a softer side and that he didn't need to act in such a foul way all the time. It can take a long time but if you are consistent and persistent, the child does eventually come to understand that you care and, though they may not admit it or even know it themselves, this is what they need more than anything in the world.

Sometimes though, it's worth forgetting to be patient, and instead, taking a risk and telling it how it is. The next story is about one of those occasions.

Almost all the young people who came to us were smokers. There was zero tolerance for drugs and alcohol but we decided quite early on that we would be on a hiding to nothing if we declared war on smoking. We made our views known. We made it clear that we didn't approve of it and we offered to support anyone who wanted to quit but we felt we had to recognise and accept that our young people were already addicted and were not going to stop until this was a choice they made for themselves. Smoking was not allowed in the unit, nor on minibuses, nor during outdoor activities. It was tolerated during breaks, always outside and as much as possible out of sight. Breaks needed to occur every hour though it depended a little on what we were doing. On longer minibus trips, or if we didn't want youngsters lighting up as soon as we arrived at an activity, we would stop en route for a break. On one of these breaks the smokers lit up behind the bus. Liz and Karen were in the front seats waiting for them to finish. Simon walked to the front to ask a question and when Karen wound down the window he blew a cloud of smoke in her face. Fixing him with her steeliest look she said, "Simon, fuck off."

None of the staff, let alone young people, had ever heard Karen swear. There was a moment's complete silence as Simon's jaw dropped before he began spluttering his outrage.

"Liz, Liz, did you hear that?"

When Liz had recovered her composure enough to suppress the laughter in her voice, she replied,

"Yes, I did. You swear all the time, Simon, so why are you so shocked? Now get in the bus. We need to go."

Simon surprised the adults by looking thoughtful.

Then he smiled. "Fair enough," he said, and got on the bus.

Simon's swearing didn't stop but it did get a lot more controlled, and we noticed that while he continued to swear a lot in front of his peers, with adults it became much more rare.

As bits of Simon's armour fell off and he dropped his shield, we began to find out more about him. Simon and Ricky had different dads. When mum split up from Simon's dad she struggled to look after the two boys. This didn't surprise us as we had found the pair of them together a real handful. Simon now lived on the edge of the city in a suburb with dad and stepmum. They had their own children and clearly found Simon very hard work. There had been frequent changes of school as he moved between his parents and a lot of time out of school because of his frequent exclusions. He was well known to the local police and had been arrested for shooting out street lamps with a BB gun. As his father and stepmum got more exasperated there was frequent talk about going into care.

What was not an option it seemed was going back to mum. This interested us because it was clear that Simon loved and hero-worshipped his elder brother. On one occasion he talked about how he had visited Ricky in hospital and how scared he was that he was going to die. It was very moving to listen to - heart breaking even. There was no doubt that Simon would have been very happy to live with Ricky again. Why didn't it happen? Was it just that the two of them together would be too much of a handful?

We got an answer of sorts one day when mum came into the unit for a meeting about Ricky. Simon bounded into the office to say hello and she barely acknowledged him. Everyone in the meeting was shocked and even Ricky looked embarrassed. Simon came away crestfallen and was very quiet for the rest of the afternoon. We never did find out what lay behind this.

This incident was very revealing as unconditionality must be the one essential responsibility of a parent, just as I believe it is for anyone choosing to work with troubled children. If you have your own child you don't give up on them no matter what they do. Anything less is emotional abuse.

It's easy to say but does it also apply when the parents are barely more than children? Teenage parents, like Ricky was to become within a year or so of leaving us, need a huge amount of support. I'm sure Ricky loved his baby son but was he any more equipped for parenthood than his own parents had been? These are questions society has to start addressing if we are ever to move beyond continually having to rescue vulnerable troubled children.

Simon stayed with us to the end of Year 9 and then was moved onto a different alternative provision where he would get more academic input than we were able to give him. We were not convinced that this is what he most needed. He had wanted to join the army but sadly a few years later we heard he had been in prison.

If we thought we'd seen the last of this troubled family we were wrong. Another one appeared! This was Kieran who was a much gentler and quieter version of his elder brothers. We were certain Ricky had been living on his own with mum but now here was Kieran and at meetings we were seeing mum again. What's more we discovered there were also younger children at home. Had they all previously been in care and then returned to mum? It was hard to see why Kieran had ended up being excluded from school. Perhaps he just expected to follow in his brothers' footsteps?

With some troubled families history just seemed to endlessly repeat itself. We do need a 'troubled families programme' but not as an austerity measure to cut the welfare budget in the medium term. It is not a simple problem. It requires a well thought-out, long term strategy that is applied with persistence and consistency.

5 Adrian

endless chances

From the start Liz and I knew what we wanted to achieve with Respect4us. We wanted children to have space to be themselves, and time in which to grow up. They had to learn to trust us and know that we were never going to give up on them. They could have as many chances as they needed. In recruiting staff we were looking for people who would not instinctively opt for coercion when faced with defiance. If threats and sanctions were ever going to work with these young people they would not have been with us in the first place.

These are easy words, but to put them into practice requires phenomenal effort. When people do things that make us feel personally insulted, threatened, intimidated, or attacked, the natural human response is defence, perhaps meeting aggression with aggression. Teachers, social workers, police officers and practically anyone working face to face with the public is having to handle and control these emotions on a daily basis. Even the most experienced of us - and many of our staff were very young - failed to live up to these standards from time to time.

The key tool for training our staff and developing the culture we wanted, was our end-of-day staff meeting. I will mention this frequently because it was the most important daily activity bearing on our success.

Adrian's story is about some of these issues.

It was a busy lunchtime in King's Lynn and the market square had been packed with people, heading for the shops and market stalls, or just away from their workplaces to get something to eat. Jason and Donna had agreed to go in to get the chips. I said I'd stay outside with the group. At the last minute Adrian had gone inside too. For a drizzly wet day it was incredibly busy with throngs of people all around us. My head kept swivelling left and right to keep an eye on our young people who were beginning to drift away into the crowds.

Then I heard Adrian.

Everyone heard Adrian.

For a second or two I was confused and couldn't think.

What had happened?

Adrian watched the gob of spit trickle down the shop window. No one inside had noticed! Rage subsumed him.

"GIVE ME MY CHIPS YOU FUCKERS," he roared, before again spitting with as much force as he could muster against the window.

Now he had their attention. The three chip shop staff had stopped whatever they were doing and were staring at him through the window with wide eyes and slack jaws. Jason and Donna, who were at the head of the queue and were just being served, having initially glanced at him, were now looking at the floor.

He started to fill his lungs ready to yell again. He felt my hand on his shoulder and shrugged it off.

"GIVE ME MY CHIPS…" he felt my hand again, more firmly, and twisted to knock it away.

"I WANT MY CHIPS.. .. "

"Adrian…. STOP….. NOW!...... and calm down."

I realised I was no longer hemmed in by the crowd. Shifting my focus from Adrian for a split second I looked around. There was now five metres of space all around me but beyond that the crowd was thicker than ever. Every face in the crowd was focussed on me and Adrian.

At last the adrenalin kicked in and I became fully alert. I fixed Adrian with my death stare.

"Keep calm. Your chips are just coming. Jason is….."

But Adrian was already turning back for another assault on the shop window.

"GIVE ME MY.."

38

Inside I could see that Jason had the attention of the shop staff and had clearly convinced them that the only way this nightmare was going to end was if they finished serving him. They moved quickly and within seconds Jason and Donna were on the street with armfuls of hot wrapped chip packets.

"Let's go, everyone," I called, and pushed my way into the throng of rubber-necked bystanders, which yielded in front of me surprisingly easily. I turned to check if I was leading anyone. Good, most were following the chips. Donna was rounding up the stragglers. And Adrian? With one last mighty gob at the shop window, he turned and followed too.

Liz, who had not been on the trip, chaired the meeting that evening.
"So, what led up to all this?" she asked.
"It was a horrible wet day, so we skipped the walk we were going to do through the historical town," said Jason.
"We went straight to the museum,"added Donna.
"Which was a disaster," I said. "Wet day. It was packed. We couldn't keep the kids together and they ran amok."
"I found Shane climbing on one of the exhibits,"said Jason.
"It was one of those days when you'd just like to start again with a different plan," I said. "We made a quick decision to call it a day, get back to the minibus and return to base."
"But first we went to get chips for lunch," said Donna, "which we'd agreed we were going to do as we'd left without a packed lunch."
"I stayed outside with the kids, while Jason and Donna went into the chip shop to get 12 lots of chips," I said. "But Adrian went too."
"Long queue in the shop," said Jason. "Adrian was bleating about wanting something different and I told him it was complicated enough and he should wait outside. That's when he spat on the floor."
"The girl behind the counter noticed and said something to her boss, who told Adrian to not behave like an animal in his shop," said Donna. "I don't think the guy realised Adrian was with us or he might have spoken to us instead."

"Adrian went mad," said Jason. "Called the poor man a 'fucking cunt', and spat on the floor again. The bloke said he wasn't serving him and he was to get out of the shop or he was calling the cops. That's when I butted in, told Adrian to get out fast and he'd lost the chance to have any chips. Knowing Adrian, I was quite surprised that he did actually go."

"Then he kicked off outside," I joined in. "I was unaware of what had gone on in the shop so it was all out of the blue and I was really confused," I said. "We headed straight for the minibus and ate the chips there, out of the rain. He did have his chips - in the interest of peace - and he was very quiet on the way home."

"OK" said Liz. "So one of those days. We probably shouldn't have headed out in the first place. Given the weather, the plan should have been scrapped and a wet weather alternative decided on. We learn for the next time. No town centres for a bit... or museums, while there are so many tourists about. So Adrian lost it. We know he can do that. Were we ready for it? How well did we handle it? What do you think the consequences for Adrian should be?"

Consequences? Reading this you are probably thinking Adrian is a pretty disgusting human being. If you've stuck with the book this far you are unlikely to be someone who thinks that things like this didn't happen when we still had corporal punishment in schools. Of course, there are many people who do think exactly that. And they probably also favour capital punishment. You, Reader, will have worked out by now that nobody could work at Respect and be thinking that way. However, after experiencing a really bad day like this one, it's understandable that none of us were feeling particularly sympathetic to Adrian. Donna, Jason and I all thought he'd embarrassed us, ruined the day for everyone, and he deserved the most serious penalty available to us. This was to stop him attending for a few days. Obviously, various things go with that, such as his school being informed, carers being spoken to, and Adrian himself having to hear how disappointed we all were, with an apology being expected when he came back. It doesn't sound very much, but we took exclusion very seriously, and it was the most extreme consequence we could apply. Generally, it worked. The young people at Respect liked us and they liked attending. Believe it or not most of them recognised that they were getting a good deal from Respect, and appreciated that they were getting another chance. They didn't want to be shut out. They might not have admitted it but none of them wanted to be excluded.

So, all agreed? Adrian was to be excluded.
"Er...No," said Liz.
"What? No?"
"You had a bad day and you are not going to make Adrian the scapegoat. None of you are in the mood to talk about it right now, so we'll all sleep on it over the weekend and talk about it again on Monday morning," said Liz, quietly but firmly.

Liz was so annoying sometimes!
...... but as usual she was right.

So, why should anyone feel any sympathy for Adrian?

He was thirteen, a child. His mother was an alcoholic and drug user who throughout Adrian's life had had unsuitable partner after unsuitable partner. Adrian loved his mum and every so often, when she was having a new attempt at getting her life in order, she would have Adrian to live with her again. The rest of the time he lived with his grandparents. They were kindly people who meant well but they lacked parenting skills and no longer had the energy to cope with a troubled teenager. Adrian had been neglected all his life and on the rare occasions the adults in his life noticed him, they tended to spoil him. There had been virtually no consistency in his rearing. If he behaved sometimes like a petulant two year old, could it really be considered his fault?

Fortunately Adrian had a really good social worker. She had been his case worker for some time and knew him well. Adrian liked her as did we. Children's services are massively over-worked, laughably under-paid, at risk all the time of being

41

pilloried when things go wrong and it's therefore no surprise that there is a high turnover of staff and little consistency for the children who need it the most. So in this matter Adrian was lucky.

He was also lucky in his high school, as the teacher who managed special educational needs had taken Adrian under his wing and given him a massive amount of pastoral support. This teacher had got to know the family and the social worker and had begun the painstaking work of unpicking some of Adrian's learned behaviours. However, the school was in the process of becoming an academy and as such was increasingly focused on exam results and league table position. Adrian's champion, able to see the writing on the wall, had found the funding to send him to Respect, hoping we would be able to continue the work he had begun.

Was Adrian grateful? Of course not! He arrived angry, defensive and with a very thick protective shield which he was going to allow no one through. For the staff, it was very hard to find any common ground or any activity that looked as though it might engage him. He was resistant and actively disruptive to whatever activity was taking place.

It was Liz who made the breakthrough. She describes what happened:
"We were never ones to give up easily and he certainly tested us! One day we had a first aid course running which he delighted in trying to sabotage along with another lad. I took them both out into another room where Denise was doing art with a small group. We had a cup of tea and joined in with the art project. I was sitting alongside him and suddenly he started to talk. Denise, always the brilliant team worker, realised immediately what was going on and removed the other kids to the far end of the room to give us some space. He had begun by talking about his brothers and how they didn't get on with mum. And then there was this flood of sadness mixed with anger as all sorts of detail of family history came out. Gradually in front of me this obnoxious teenager was transformed into a very worried and

42

frightened child. It was so clear to me that he needed space and time to heal and to learn to trust. For this to happen our support for him had to be unfailing and unconditional."

From then onwards Liz and Denise were Adrian's great supporters no matter what! He continued to be foul, disruptive and vicious and Liz found herself constantly advocating on his behalf to the rest of the team. So when she had asked us to sleep over the weekend on the decision to exclude, it was not unexpected. And sure enough on Monday morning we each acknowledged that perhaps we had been a little hasty. Liz undertook to talk to Adrian and by the end of the day he had apologised to each of us. This was a very big step forward. So the incident was forgotten about and we all moved on.

Before long we discovered the activity that worked best with Adrian. He loved fishing which he had learnt about from his grandad. It was an activity that he was prepared to share with others. Fishing trips with a small group including Adrian became a regular activity. Adrian would help organise them, checking equipment, finding bait and selecting venues. He would help others to set up their rods and teach them patiently how to fish. Staff who had wanted to murder him at times saw a completely different side to him. They saw a young man who could sit quietly for hours on a river bank and who could be organised, mature and responsible.

His relationship with Liz was the key to his success. He used to borrow her jacket and delight in wiping his disgusting hands on it, leaving smeary marks, after he'd been handling fish or maggots. If anyone protested he'd respond by telling them that Liz didn't mind. And he was right, she didn't! She simply put the jacket in the washing machine so it was clean for him the next time he wanted to borrow it.

In this way Adrian began to trust and to feel accepted.

In Year 10 he went back into school full time. He still had his bad days and periods of non-attendance but he completed school, went to college and into work.

6 Grandad

experiencing achievement

Some of our activities were non-negotiable - for example, the academic work at the start of the day, or lunch as a sit-down meal for everyone - but otherwise we tried to give our young people as much autonomy over their activities as possible. Usually this would involve talking through the day's possibilities and allowing the youngsters to decide and agree on the activity for the day. If we had a stable group attending on a particular day of the week we would sometimes take on a long-term project. The sponsored walk across Norfolk was one such project.

The biggest restraint on what we could do was lack of money. Cash flow was always a problem for our business. Respect4us operated through the years of "Austerity" from 2010 and the money available to schools got tighter and tighter. We charged schools a per head daily rate and our income fluctuated wildly through the year. We always operated on a shoestring with income barely enough to cover wages through the year. There was little left over for activities. Vannessa, our business manager, kept a tight grip on spending and made us all quake if we dared present invoices she was not expecting. As a result we were always on the look-out for engaging outdoor activities that would cost us nothing.

On Tuesdays that year we had a very diverse but stable group. Two of the oldest, and both natural leaders, were Jack and Malcolm. Malcolm was known as Grandad due to his fondness for sitting in the most comfortable armchair (no one else was allowed to use it when Grandad was around) and giving his opinion on everything that was wrong with the world. Grandad and Jack had persuaded the group that they would do a long distance walk. Both of them were trying to improve their physical fitness and the staff saw opportunities to build in learning about the environment - especially nature, wildlife, geography and local history.

There was a lot of talk, led by Jack and Grandad, about doing something memorable like a marathon and raising money for a charity. A number of walks were suggested that could be done as the weather permitted and that would take up much of the year. Eventually they decided to do the Weavers' Way, a 61 mile footpath across Norfolk from Cromer to Yarmouth. One attraction of this project for the young people was that it ended at Great Yarmouth and we had agreed to a day at the Pleasure Beach if the walk was completed. This would prove invaluable later on as we referred to it regularly when morale was flagging. There was then discussion about sponsorship and the cause we might support. Jack had recently lost his grandfather to heart disease and Grandad's grandfather also suffered from heart problems. Sanjay told us how his uncle had had a heart attack as he stepped off the plane from India. All of this tied in with discussions about walking being such a healthy activity for your heart. The group decided unanimously that the money they raised should go to the British Heart Foundation.

The weather that autumn was lovely. The first leg of the walk was to be from Cromer to Felbrigg. The minibus dropped the group at the start of the walk by the sea in Cromer and there was excited talk about how they would have to walk 61 miles before they saw the sea again. For most there was little understanding of what the distance meant and the effort required to cover it. For all of them and for the staff this was going to be quite a challenge. Fortunately the first leg was quite a short one.

After half an hour we had left the town behind - always a relief for us as there were many more distractions and opportunities for mischief in towns - and the group began climbing stiles, opening and closing gates and trudging across fields. The footpath ran diagonally across a large field which had been sown with winter wheat. The path was narrow and not very clear having been fairly recently ploughed so the group were in single file. As they were strung out across the middle of the field a network of sprinklers suddenly sprang to life. Nothing like a drenching to turn a gentle amble into a helter-skelter run! When they arrived at the minibus all were still smiling.

46

And so the walk continued leg by leg. On the short and wet days in winter there was plenty of work to be done at the unit. A map appeared across one of the walls of the workshop room with Cromer at one side and Great Yarmouth at the other. The progress of the walk was marked with a large arrow and behind it the space filled up with photographs, diary accounts, drawings and mementoes. Other activities included producing sponsorship forms and leaflets about what we were doing. Some began doing research on heart disease, on developing fitness programmes to protect the heart, or on the places our route would take us through in the weeks ahead.

The walk was arduous and there were times when everyone felt they were never going to complete it. One section along the River Thurne from Potter Heigham was done by boat in order to break the monotony of endless walking. One assumes that kids in a county like Norfolk will have done all these things but we discovered very few of them had been on a boat before. They are city kids and some of them had not been out of Norwich before joining Respect. It was shocking to realise that for one or two a trip into the city centre was a rare event and that they scarcely ever left their estate or immediate neighbourhood.

The boat had a maximum speed of 4mph, and was so robust no one could do any damage to it. Jason was in his element on the river and he took charge as each of the youngsters drove the boat. The course was erratic as they all tried to steer the boat (pronounced "boot" in Norfolk dialect) to hit any passing ducks. Jason told them they would never succeed but it didn't stop them trying. As well as ducks they managed to avoid hitting any other craft and the day passed without any of the great mishaps that the more fearful members of staff had predicted. All agreed that boating was a lot more fun than walking and were disappointed that they were not allowed to continue by boat all the way to Yarmouth.

Another distraction to keep them occupied on the walk was to bring a dog. They managed to persuade Vannessa to lend them

47

her Staffordshire terrier called Duke which she occasionally brought into work. Although an extremely hot day in early summer, it should have been a simple and pleasant stroll beside the River Bure. Unfortunately a large section of the path was closed for repairs to the river bank and there was a very long diversion, in the course of which the navigators took a wrong turn, the diversion signs having disappeared. At one point they ended up in a campsite where a big commotion was taking place with plenty of flashing lights from ambulances and police cars. This was all much more interesting and entertaining for young people than endless walking. They had to be dragged away but later they checked out what had been going on and discovered someone had died as result of severe burns incurred when they lit a stove inside a tent. That began an impromptu lesson about the perils of fire and camping to make sure they were never tempted to do the same.

By now everyone was very hot and bothered and losing all confidence in their navigators as they pushed on along muddy paths through reed beds. Duke had long since decided he had had enough and was having to be carried in turns by the older boys. Eventually they found themselves back on the river and I was there to meet them. I had parked the minibus and walked quite some distance before I came across them. I had come prepared with a ruck sack full of drinks and snacks but was still moaned at because the walk had been so hard. Once they had consumed refreshments they were a little happier and wanted to know where the minibus was parked. Despair returned when they discovered they still had to walk several miles back to where I'd parked the bus.

At the staff debriefing at the end of the day we decided that although it might have been character building, no one wanted to go through that again. In future we would check beforehand that there were no path closures and check out all the alternative routes. At least one member of staff would have to be a skilled map navigator.

Vannessa later reported that Duke had slept for two days solid and would now bury his head under his paws whenever she got his lead out. He never came on a walk with us again.

The final stretch along Breydon Water into Great Yarmouth was a marathon as there is no road access to the path for about ten miles of the route. But by now the group was showing plenty of resilience and were determined to finish and glimpse the sea again having walked all the way across Norfolk. They were amazingly supportive and encouraging of each other. Getting into Yarmouth was a real team effort.

The reward the following week was a whole day at the Pleasure Beach. While going on the rides was an experience most of them had had before, never had they felt they had earned their treat as much as on this occasion. It was a lovely finish to a great project. But it was not quite over. The last step was to get someone in from the British Heart Foundation to receive a cheque for the money they had raised. That person turned out to be a very attractive young woman to whom Jack and Grandad paid solicitous attention. She thanked all the group for the effort they had put in.

We were very pleased with the walk as a project. It had gone on for a long time - most of the academic year, - and the young people had sustained their interest in it. It taught them about long term planning, commitment and sticking at something until it was finished. It gave them a sense of achievement few of them had experienced before.

All these young people - Grandad, Jack, Sanjay - struggled in school and got themselves into trouble. They needed time and space - a breather from school. At school they felt like failures. They left Respect proud of what they had achieved. After college Grandad got a job and now has a family. Sanjay went to university and is now running the family business.

7 Mathew
identity

Schools try really hard to be inclusive but some children are so different they make it hard for any social group to include them. Mathew was one of these. Even at Respect we had difficulty fitting him in. At every turn he was awkward. We knew he was in care and lived in a children's home but that was all we knew about him and he chose to tell us little more.

His story starts beside a roundabout on a fast road just outside Great Yarmouth.

"You can never afford to relax as a member of staff at Respect," I thought to myself, as, wincing and flinching, I observed cars on the roundabout, horns blaring, swerving left and right, braking to avoid a teenage youth erratically zig-zagging across the carriageways.

I'd been on "Mathew Duty" all day. This involved sticking like a limpet to Mathew.
Why me?
"You have an aptitude for it," Liz said.
"You have more patience than us," Jason said.
"You're a good listener."
"Mathew interests you."
"You're the only member of staff that doesn't want to strangle him."
"Mathew likes you and sometimes does what you tell him," they said.
I didn't swallow any of this flattery but it was obvious the staff had agreed among themselves that Mathew was my job and I was to have no say in the matter.

Mathew had a very direct stare that freaked out the other kids. He had long periods of silence where he would just observe…. and stare. For an adult, even when you suspect it's all an act, it could still be a little scary until you got to know him. Mathew never gave the other young people at Respect a chance to get to know him.

I was always amazed at how broad-minded our young people were. They were unhesitatingly tolerant and accepting of other races, of gays and of people who were different to them. They were genuinely shocked and appalled by racism, sexism and homophobia. They were curious about other people and could ask very direct questions which could sometimes be interpreted as offensive but offence was rarely intended. Unlike many children in normal schools they were used to change and difference. Some had been through several schools, lived with different families, moved around the county, some around the country. They'd had more than their share of nasty and unpleasant experiences. Most had learned the value of solidarity. On arriving at Respect they were quick to form a group, to support one another and were welcoming to newcomers. But newcomers had to make an effort, and Mathew never did. He made it clear that he was a loner. This didn't mean he wanted to be ignored. He seemed to want to shock the other young people and he clearly wanted adult attention. A very complex character!

He had arrived this week with bleached hair, some dyed purple and some green. Today he had his guitar and was playing me a song he said he had written the night before. I was really impressed though I found out later it was a song in the charts that almost anyone apart from me would have recognised. After listening to Mathew singing we got deep into a discussion about gender reassignment. For a number of weeks Mathew had been telling me that he was transsexual. Now he maintained that his social worker had agreed that he could have reassignment surgery. I asked what this involved and Mathew seemed to have quite a detailed knowledge which he was keen to share. I listened, nodding to show Mathew that he still had my attention, while over his shoulder scanning the unit to keep an eye on what was happening elsewhere.

The others had all finished their maths and English work and switched to playing pool and competing on video games. Noise levels were rising. One or two were helping Liz and Vannessa put a packed lunch together in the kitchen. Some older ones had disappeared outside, while a couple of younger boys were charging from room to room. The adults exchanged glances.

"OK time to go," called Liz, "All onto the bus."

We cleared the unit, rounding up the group who had spread in all directions, and began to herd them onto the minibus. Mathew remained seated.

"Come on Mattie. It's time to go."

"Nah, Dom, I'm staying here today."

"Not an option, mate. We are all out today."

"Vannessa's not going. I'll stay with her."

"Vannessa's got work to do. Business stuff. She's got no time to supervise you. Anyway we'll get some exercise and have fun. It'll be good, you'll see. I want to carry on with what we were talking about. It was really interesting."

"But I've got my guitar. I'm not leaving it."

"Well, bring it too if you don't mind carrying it while we are on the walk. Or you can leave it on the bus."

"I'm not leaving it anywhere."

"That's ok but we need to go now. The others are all waiting on the bus."

"For fuck's sake…." Mathew leapt up, grabbed the guitar and stormed out of the unit. He went straight to the front passenger door, pulled himself and the guitar up onto the seat and slammed the door behind him. He knew he was not supposed to ride in the front.

"Just let him be," I thought. "Please, may no one comment or start complaining about Mathew getting away with things." I climbed in the side door and slid it shut behind myself.

At the woods everyone clambered out of the bus. Mathew remained seated.

"Come on Mattie. You'll enjoy it when you get going. We all need the exercise."

There was no response.

I said to Liz, "Leave me the keys. You go on. We'll catch you up."

52

When the last of the group had disappeared round the first bend in the path, Mathew got out of the bus. I locked the door.

"We are going to have to hurry to catch them up."

Mathew sat down on a log and began strumming his guitar.

"Do you want to talk about it? Why don't you want to go with the others?"

Silence.

"Well I want to walk. You're welcome to join me and we can talk along the way."

I started walking up the path thinking Mathew would probably give in and follow. At the bend I turned round to check. Mathew was no longer sitting on the log and was nowhere to be seen.

"Where is he?" I thought. "He is so annoying!"

I stood still, watching for any sign of movement. Nothing. I ambled back down the path, eyes scanning the forest on each side. Mathew had done his Houdini trick again!

"Should have known better," I thought. "I shouldn't have taken my eyes off him."

So what is the secret to managing this disturbed boy's behaviour? I sat down on the log vacated by Mathew to have a think about what to do. I had about an hour before the others would return. He wouldn't have gone far… and he always turned up again. It's just how long would he keep us all waiting? The other kids would have no patience and could turn into a lynch mob. We only had the one vehicle so we couldn't split up. Should I phone Vannessa for support? That would be a last resort. Meanwhile I needed to see if I could find him. I should check the road first, down at the entrance to the forest - make sure he's not attempting to leave the site.

I walked down the track towards the main road. Relief! There he was, sitting on a forestry gate. Seeing me, he started strumming the guitar again.

Feigning equal disinterest, I decided to keep my distance. I sat on a tree stump, staring into the forest, but all the time watching out of the corner of my eye.

After ten minutes or so, Mathew shambled up the track and found a seat a little distance away. Not a word was said by either of us. Mathew began strumming the guitar again.

After a few minutes I said,

"Can you play and sing the one I heard this morning - that lovely song you wrote last night? I really liked that one."

The strumming stopped. He cleared his throat, played a few bars and then began singing.

When he had finished I said,

"That's amazing Mattie. You could go professional. I'll be your manager. We'd split everything fifty-fifty."

I was rewarded with a half smile!

"Eighty-twenty," Mathew said.

"Sixty-forty"

"Seventy-thirty"

"DONE!" I shouted.

We fist bumped.

We began talking about how life would be as a famous pop star. If he was famous would it be easier or more difficult to be trans? What would his life be like? What would he enjoy about life and what would be difficult or unpleasant? How would it all be different to his present life?

We were just getting on to talk about what he'd change in his current life and how he might start to do that when I heard the noise of the walking group back at the bus and Liz calling. We walked back together, still talking. As I handed over the keys I exchanged glances with Liz and winked at her raised eyebrow. The group piled into the bus. This time Mathew went into the back. The walking group had been really good, said Liz, but they were thirsty, so please could we stop to get cold drinks?

The first pit stop was alongside a busy main road in a car park off a large roundabout. Liz parked and I went in to get the drinks. From inside I glanced through the window and noticed Liz racing across the car park towards the road. With my eyes I followed her direction of travel and projected forward to the road. There was Mathew walking calmly across the carriageway looking neither to left nor right, cars passing to the front and the rear of him, horns blaring. Leaving the drinks I raced outside. The group were standing around the minibus, jaws hanging, eyes riveted to the drama developing. Mathew was now on the other side off the road heading off behind the roundabout.

"Get in!" I shouted. "Lets go and get him"

The youngsters piled in. Liz was returning across the car park. We stopped for her and then headed back onto the carriageway.

"Where is he?" I thought, as I steered right around the roundabout.

"Can anyone see which way he went?"

The car in front swerved to the side, and suddenly there he was in front of us, strolling across the carriageway and onto the roundabout.

"Everyone, keep your eyes on him."

We continued round to find him crossing again in front of us on the far side of the roundabout. I pulled into the left beside him. Liz opened the front passenger door and to everyone's surprise he climbed in. The rest of the group all started abusing him. I yelled at them to shut up and set off. As we got going Mathew suddenly opened the front passenger door. He was still seat-belted and clearly had no intention of going anywhere. Liz reached across and pulled it shut.

"This is all just to shock," I thought, "but nonetheless I'm not going to let it happen again."

I pulled in and Liz swapped seats with him to guard the door.

Liz then began a discussion by asking the group what name they would choose for themselves if they were to change gender. Everyone seemed relieved to have something light to think about after the tension of the previous ten minutes. If, as I thought, Mathew's aim all along was to shock, then this discussion underlined that nobody was shocked by him, not staff, not young people. We talked about him being trans as though it was the most ordinary thing in the world. While we had been shocked by him putting himself in such danger on the road, we had pretended we weren't and had underlined it by the calm way we had coped.

We reviewed the situation at our end of day meeting. The resulting list of jobs was a long one. We would need to re-visit our risk assessment, talk to the children's home, and write a report for them. Could we…?, should we….? keep Mathew on? We couldn't have a repeat of that day but if he remained with us no one could guarantee that it wouldn't happen again. But none of us wanted to give up on him. We were talking with him, observing and increasing our understanding of him all the time. He was not a hopeless case.

The decision was taken out of our hands when Mathew went to live in a different children's home and it proved too difficult to get him to us in Norwich. We were not clear about where he finished his schooling but we know he went on to further education. He came to see us a few years later. While still a rather strange young man he seemed happy, was in work and leading a productive life. He had not had a sex change.

8 Carol and Hannah

teenage pregnancy

Teenage girls have been getting pregnant forever. The UK has the highest teen pregnancy rate in Western Europe. In England in 2018 there were 2413 pregnancies in girls under 16. 926 of these went through to term and a live birth. There were a further 1037 babies born to 16 year old girls.[3] With approximately 3500 secondary schools in England, the average school should reasonably be expecting one pregnancy a year. For a school serving a deprived area of the country at least one pregnancy a year is a near certainty. Despite these facts, schools are strangely unprepared for this eventuality.

Pregnant girls are no longer publicly shamed, cast out and rejected by society as they used to be not so long ago. There is no longer a religious based condemnation, apart perhaps within some minority cultures. However this has been replaced by a twenty-first century popular intolerance. Young people are supposedly too stupid or too reckless to learn from the sex and health education they are provided with and to use the contraception that is freely available to them. Girls shouldn't get pregnant. And it's illegal. These teen parents are imagined to be living the life of Riley at the taxpayers' expense. To provide facilities, to set out to take care of them, would only encourage more of it.

Against these views is the argument that we know it is going to happen whether we like it or not and without support, more than one young life is going to be ruined. The children of teenage parents themselves experience lower educational attainment and are at risk of lower economic activity and social disadvantage as adults. As with all these issues, the more we intervene with support, the more likely we are to break the cycle of deprivation.

---

[3] Office for National Statistics

In my experience there are very few teenagers who make a conscious decision to have a baby. For most it is a mistake, and a mistake for which they will pay a very heavy personal price even in our enlightened times. It is also the case that most teenage pregnancies are among girls in the most poor and deprived areas of cities and regions of the country; and if it's a function of deprivation then perhaps, as with so many issues, we need to look to reduce inequality as the most effective way of eliminating teenage pregnancy.

There is some good news. In the last twenty years in the UK, the conception rate among under 16s has fallen by more than half. With good pastoral support and a few basic facilities there really is no reason why girls shouldn't continue to study throughout their pregnancy. But the reality is that most girls who get pregnant do not finish school. They vanish as far as schools are concerned. They get picked up by the local authority and continue an education of sorts with alternative provision.

At Respect4us we had a number of young mums over the years. The following two case studies put a human face to the statistics.

The first is one of those very few cases where a conscious decision had been made to have a baby. Carol and Ian had been in a relationship for more than a year. She was 15 and he was 16 when she got pregnant. Professionals of all sorts had had their say and their advice had been steadfastly rejected. This couple knew their own mind. They wanted a family together. Both came from chaotic and insecure family backgrounds themselves. All their emotional support came from one another and they had been in a very stable relationship since their early teens. Now they wanted a baby of their own to love.

Ian continued in school but Carol stopped attending and Children's Services asked us to take her on. Donna was her key worker and she gave her constant attention and support. Together they talked through all of Carol's hopes and fears. She had very low levels of literacy and we set to work to improve that. She desperately wanted to do the very best she could for her baby, so she had incentives to work hard that she had never had before. We built a curriculum for her around literacy and child care. Her attendance was good and she began to make real progress with learning.

Then after a twenty-two week scan her baby had a diagnosis of spina bifida. If she survived to term the baby would need surgery and then face many life-threatening issues - and with a mother who was herself only a child. Of course Carol was offered a termination, and she refused. For Respect4us, supporting Carol through all this seemed like an awesome responsibility. We took the decision not to try to influence her in any way at all. She was under enough pressure as it was. We made it clear we would support her in whatever she wanted to do. We went back to studying childcare with her but now with the focus on learning everything we could about spina bifida.

When the baby was born she survived just long enough for both parents to hold her. We were all traumatised by this tragedy but Donna bore the brunt of it. She was invited to the funeral but couldn't find the strength to make herself go. However, she made regular visits to see Carol and supported her to come back and finish her year. The day Carol came in she had a big smile on her face and was genuinely pleased to see us all again. We all felt this appallingly disadvantaged but amazingly brave and tough young girl deserved rather better from life.

Ian got an apprenticeship and they got their own home together. By the time Carol was seventeen she had another baby who was healthy and seemed to be thriving. Liz bumped into her in a local supermarket and got an update on how they were getting on. Ian was in work and Carol was thinking about having more babies.

The statistics say the young family was unlikely to stay together and there would be poor educational outcomes for the children. Who really knows? Certainly this couple knew their own minds and had shown themselves totally impervious to the opinions of others. They needed no one's approval. They had been dealt a very poor hand in life but were determined to find happiness through making the most of what little was available to them.

The other young mum, Hannah, was referred to us directly from a local school. She was 14 and came with a small army of social workers, health care assistants, nurses, midwives, police officers and lawyers, all of whom visited for appointments with her from time to time. As usual we asked no questions but it was very obvious that this was a high profile case with someone heading to court for the rape of a minor. For us it was enough to know that as well as being pregnant, Hannah had suffered and was continuing to suffer from plenty of trauma.

Despite all this she settled in with us very easily. She liked that we didn't put her under any pressure, that we took her pregnancy seriously and adapted our routines and activities to meet her needs. She had found school almost impossible because of the attitudes she faced and because nothing really changed to accommodate her. A few of the boys we had with us at the time were a little judgemental but this was easily dealt with. Hannah herself helped us to educate them by being prepared to talk about her experience of being pregnant.

We helped Hannah to relax ensuring she had somewhere to sit or lie down and take naps whenever she needed. She was a very bright girl, clearly able academically and had high aspirations. The school was still doing some distance learning with her so we concentrated on practical skills. Denise taught her sewing and cooking and Jason worked with her on art at which she was very good, and which she found very therapeutic.

Hannah's mum was a great asset and was totally supportive of her. Mun blamed herself for not having observed that her daughter was being groomed and was determined to make amends by doing everything she possibly could to make sure Hannah's life was not completely ruined by what had happened.

The court case was an horrendous experience for Hannah. We asked no questions but were always there to listen. We had activities lined up to distract her but she was under no pressure to do any of them. Jason had become her key worker helping her with art and woodwork. Together they designed and built items she might need for the baby - a cradle and mobiles. They drew and painted together. We thought it really important that through Jason's kindness, gentleness, reliability and concern for her we could demonstrate to her that not all adult men were self-seeking and untrustworthy. Eventually Hannah's sunny side returned and we knew she was going to be ok.

She had always been clear to us that she wanted to go on to college and complete her education as well as looking after her baby. However we knew that she was dreading going back to school for her final year and GCSE's. Fortunately this was not going to be necessary as the school arranged for her to complete her GCSE courses at the college. We helped her to become familiar with the college and to research and organise childcare, travel and all the details of her life as a student.

Hannah had a perfectly healthy baby whom she brought back to meet us all. She went to college, she completed her exam courses and then went on to study A levels.

We admired these two young women immensely for their courage and strength of character. While they weren't even halfway through their teens they had coped with more trauma than most of us have to handle in a lifetime. We thought they were utterly amazing.

9 Millie

neglect and drugs

This one is another story about a child from a "troubled family". Millie was bright and clever, with a sweet, and utterly charming personality. But for the accident of birth she could have done anything with her life.

Her story begins with Liz talking to her mother in the family's living room, waiting for Millie to get out of bed.

"Mrs Drake, it's probably not a good idea to let Millie smoke weed at home", said Liz as she and Millie's mum waited for the girl to finish getting dressed upstairs.

Mrs Drake managed to raise her eyebrows, roll her eyes upwards and fix Liz with an evil stare all at the same time.
"What? You reckon if I tell her not to smoke dope she's going to do what I tell her? You think if I actually managed to get her not to smoke at home she's not going to do it everywhere else she goes? Do I have to chuck her out? And all her brothers? And her stepdad? Do you know what most of the other kids around here are taking? And you're worried about her doing weed? For fucks sake, isn't there enough trouble in the world without making a fuss about nothing?!"

She turned away from Liz in contempt.

Everyone at Respect loved Millie. She was smart, interested in everything and everyone, bubbly and full of fun. Her sense of humour was infectious. She treated us all as though we were family, constantly teasing, especially the younger male members of staff, as though they were big brothers. She was just a very relaxed person, never inappropriate, never unkind. She was up for every challenge the staff could throw at her and there would be a huge shout of triumph and laughter once the task set was achieved. Her art work was amazing and she could work quietly

62

on it for hours. Sometimes it would be portraits, soft gentle sketches and at other times startlingly disturbing paintings.

Clearly she would never have been with us in the first place if there weren't issues, and gradually these began to emerge. After the initial enthusiasm for being at Respect her attendance became more variable. Increasingly we had to go round to get her out of bed. Often there would be no response when the home was phoned. Friends were made with a kindly neighbour who could be phoned before the minibus set off and this lady would go round and yell for Millie through the letterbox. If her home life hadn't been so chaotic she might have stood a better chance. She was simply lost and vulnerable.

Things got worse when she fell for an older boy who was into harder drugs than Millie was used to. She came in one day after a week when she had not been seen at all. The group was going ice skating but she looked so ill we thought about sending her home. In the end we felt she would be safer if we let her sleep wrapped up on a sofa. The gossip from one of the other young people was that she had taken LSD and had a bad trip the night before. When she woke up Liz had a gentle but very firm talk to her. Millie agreed she needed to stop and change the direction of her life but it was clear that the minute she was taken home she would start again. Of course it was reported to the school and all the relevant agencies. The concerns were logged but everyone knew it wasn't going to make a difference until she wanted to stop. All we could do was continue to listen to her, be there for her, carry on setting her challenges, suggesting to her different directions in which she could take her life. It is so hard watching someone slowly self-destruct, wanting to pick them up and shake them, but knowing that will only drive them away.

A month went by when we didn't see her, then out of the blue, she called and asked for a lift. She was very subdued but things seemed better. She didn't want to talk about where she had been or what had happened.

Millie found a new friend at Respect in a girl called Ellie and the two became soul sisters. Some of the joy and laughter returned though they were not altogether good as a pair! Ellie was determined to fight the world and dying her hair pink was just the start. Ellie's story was similar to Millie's. When she talked of her family Liz would want to wrap her arms around her and make it all better. There were times when she seemed so sad and would want to talk, then just seemed to shake herself off, smile, and immediately get up to something she shouldn't. Ellie and Millie were great together when they weren't being bad together!

It was hard to refuse these two anything. Towards the end of their final year they talked Liz into repeating a trip to the local theme park. Liz tells the story:

"Now you would think we would have got the sniffer dogs out, made them sign behaviour agreements, asked a member of staff to stay with them all day, or even not taken them, but we didn't do any of this, we just took them along.

I smiled when they called from one of the rides, laughed with them as we all went on a ride and kept them in sight most of the time.

It was time to go home. I got everyone together except those two. Alarm bells began to ring. Nicky said she had last seen them on the lake and she had told them to bring their boat in. Sure enough they were still out in their boat. From the giggling they were clearly stoned. They openly explained they'd just found a bit in a pocket and as it was a lovely day thought they would get a "boot" and chill!

I made them sit together with me on the way home and tried to give them a stern look. Millie got off at her stop, gave me a hug and said, 'Chill out Lizzie!'

Of course I will Millie! Why wouldn't I?"

During their time at Respect many, many battles were fought with and for both girls. They never lied about the drugs they took nor the blokes they got involved with and the messes they frequently got into. They knew that we would be there for them and would always do what we could to support them. They also

64

knew they would be told off. The normal policy was to send home any who came in under the influence of drugs and drink. But for these two 'home' wasn't always the safest place to be and we felt, on balance, it was better to keep them with us where at least we could feed them, get them clean clothes if necessary, and just make them feel wanted and loved.

It would be wonderful to think there were happy outcomes for both these lovely girls. When they went off into the world, we had made sure they knew where to turn for support, and we had got them college places, but without self-motivation and without support, it's doubtful that they attended.

10 Danny

exploring boundaries

All the young people who came to us had different needs. We listened to all of them, we observed them closely, and we talked a great deal as a staff about what their needs were. The approach we took with each of them was always tailored to the individual.

Danny was a bit of a show-off and a bit of a bully. He had learned to get his own way by throwing his weight around, and by acting the fool. Eventually, this had got him excluded from school. Danny, we decided, needed to have clear boundaries set, and when he overstepped them, the opportunity to talk through what had happened and understand the consequences of his actions for himself and others.

Danny's story starts as I was driving a full minibus back from a history field trip to West Norfolk.

I looked again at my wing mirror. Why do I always assume they're after me? Does everyone else feel the same way or is it just me that always feels guilty? In the mirror I watched as, far back, the blue flashing light pulled out again into a gap in the on-coming traffic. There was a long line of traffic behind us and in front was a heavily laden cement truck which the minibus was never going to get past on this stretch of the A47. Never mind, I thought, it's not so far to the dual carriageway around Swaffham. Even this old bus should be able to overtake there.

I turned my attention back to the flashing blue light. Once more I could see it in my wing mirror.
The lights were too close together for it to be an ambulance. It's a motorcycle, I realised.
Of course, I thought, it's that bike sitting watching the traffic as we left the last roundabout after King's Lynn. Still feeling guilty, I mentally ran through all the vehicle checks. Doors all closed, no indicators flashing, 38mph and no danger of having been speeding while behind this truck.

I checked my rearview mirror. Everyone was still in their seat. "All still got your seat belts on?" I called back.

Donna, riding shotgun on the back seat, replied, "All OK Dom."

"Anyone done anything to annoy the police recently?" I asked tentatively.

Silence.

"Why? Are they after us?" asked Cheryl quietly. She was seated alone on the front seat because she had fallen out with her best friend, Lucy, now seated three rows back. I had been aware of her studying me as my eyes flickered regularly to the wing mirror.

Now she shouted, "Oh my god, the cops are coming. Better chuck that dope out the window, Lucy!"

"Shurrup, bitch!" came the reply.

"Don't you two start up again," warned Donna.

The motorcycle was now right behind and pulled out again for the last time.

All lights going, the rider stuck his left arm out indicating for the minibus to pull in to the side of the road. Carefully keeping my distance from the bike, I flicked the hazard lights on, braked to a gradual halt, engaged the handbrake and then switched the engine off. I slumped back in my seat, willing myself to relax. The bus behind was completely silent. I wound the window down, watching as the police officer propped his bike on its stand and then ambled over, slightly bow-legged, pulling his gloves off as he came.

"Good afternoon, Sir."

"Good afternoon, Officer."

"Would you mind stepping out of the vehicle please, Sir?"

I opened the door. I have nothing to feel guilty about, I thought, aware of the balloon that seemed to be expanding in my stomach.

I followed the policeman to the front of the bus.

"Where are you going Sir?"

"To Norwich. We're returning from a field trip to Castle Rising."

"Are you a school? Are they..... umm.... erm... normal kids?"

"Quite normal.....but what do you mean by normal, Officer."

"Are you .... like.. erm.. from a special school?"

"Ah, I see. No, we are from a unit that works with children with emotional and behavioural difficulties. Most of these children have been in normal secondary schools but been excluded for one reason or another."

"Aah, that explains it then. The boy sitting behind you, Sir. The one with blond hair. Um... is there anything particularly wrong with him, Sir?"

"Nothing particularly, Officer. Why do you ask?"

"Well, when you drove past me up the road, he lifted his middle finger to me."

"Oh, did he? That does sound like the sort of thing he might do....Would you like a word with him, Officer?"

"Yes please Sir.....if you think that appropriate."

I walked round to the sliding door at the side of the bus and pulled it open. There was still complete silence. No one had moved from their seats.

"Danny, can you get out please?"

Danny sat still, considering his options. Coming to the only conclusion possible, he eventually undid his seatbelt.

"Move!" he said to Aaron in the seat next to him.

Aaron pulled his knees up and Danny eased past him. Grabbing the handrail he swung down over the steps to the ground. I slid the door closed. With a jaunty swagger and a backwards grin to his mates, Danny followed me to the waiting policeman.

The officer stood there for a moment assessing the boy in front of him.

"You gave me the finger earlier, young man. Can you explain why you did that?"

For a moment Danny thought about denying it, but then, remembering he had an audience behind him, he decided instead to brazen it out with bravado.

" I don't like coppers," he said, looking insolently at the officer. "No one in my fam likes the filth."

"But you don't know me. Have I ever done anything to hurt you or upset you?"

"Well, you're all the same!"

"Don't you think that's a bit prejudiced?"

Danny said nothing.

Frustrated, the officer looked at me and shrugged his shoulders. I shook myself awake, realising I was actually in charge of the situation.

"Back on the bus," I said to Danny.

Glancing back I realised there were twelve faces craning through the front window. They could see the confrontation but not hear what was said. As Danny slid the door open I could hear Donna ordering then back to their seats. Danny climbed on board, cockily grinning at everyone. I closed the door and returned to the officer.

"Thank you for your patience," I said. "And thank you for taking the trouble to follow us and bring this to my attention. Working on behaviours that are going to get these kids into more and more trouble over the years is what we do. This is a good one that we can use…. And hopefully ensure that Danny learns something from it. I thought you were very tolerant."

"Well to begin with I was really annoyed. But when I caught up with you I realised that you've got your hands full haven't you? There's no point in making your job more difficult."

"Thank you, Officer. You are very understanding. This won't be the end of the matter. I'll be discussing it further with Danny and I'll be talking to his mum. He won't be out of the unit again until he's written you a letter of apology. Could I have a name and address please?"

"Of course."

The officer extracted a notebook and pen from one of the many pockets in his bulky jacket. I stood aside so this operation could be seen clearly from the bus. The officer wrote, then tore the page out and handed it to me. I studied it for a moment before slowly folding it and putting it into my top pocket.

"Thank you, Officer. We'll be in touch."

The officer returned to his bike and I went back to the driver's door. I climbed in and started up the bus without a word. For a moment there was complete silence on board.

"Was that a ticket?" asked a voice.

I said nothing.

"Dom's got a ticket" said a second voice.

"Danny you twat! You got Dom a ticket!" said a third voice.

"Hush everyone," said Donna.

I was silent, Danny was silent, and the bus remained silent all the way back to the city.

The trip had been to Castle Rising. History was what we did on Thursdays that year. On wet days we went to museums like Norwich Castle, Strangers' Hall, Time and Tide in Great Yarmouth, Swaffham and Cromer museums. But whenever possible and the weather allowed, it would be out of doors, hands-on history involving plenty of walking, re-enactments and wide games wherever practicable. We had been down into Thetford forest to the prehistoric flint workings of Grimes Graves. We'd been to Burgh Castle and talked about why the Romans had needed such a big and permanent encampment on that site. We'd studied maps to see how the topography might have changed over the past two thousand years. The siting of the camp would only make sense if Breydon water had in those days been the wide open estuary of the River Yare. If that was the case, would Great Yarmouth, built on a sandbank at the mouth of the Yare, have existed? The following week we were at Caister St Edmund to compare another Roman site, at one time the largest Roman town in East Anglia. Why would such a huge settlement fall into decay? Why did Norwich grow up as such an important city just a few miles to the north? Then we were onto castles and last week a small group had defended the walls and ramparts of Castle Acre against assault from all directions.

Today there had probably been too much travel. It was a 90 mile round trip from Norwich to Castle Rising. It was north of King's Lynn, overlooking The Wash, and built in the twelfth century. On the way out, I had told tales of how the "She-Wolf of France", Queen Isabella, had been held captive there following her fall from power. The story had everything for teenagers who might once have thought history boring. Isabella had arrived from France aged only 12 to marry the new king

Edward II. She soon discovered he was gay and over the years he had several male lovers. Eventually having produced an heir who was to become Edward III she took her own lover called Roger and together they overthrew Edward who met a very grisly end - I didn't spare them the details. When her son Edward III eventually asserted himself and killed Roger, she was banished to Castle Rising. All this led to fierce discussion and debate along the way. Is 12 too young to marry? What did the girls think? What would they do if they discovered the man they married was actually gay? Could it even happen nowadays?... in some cultures? Was Edward unpopular because he was gay, because he was ruthless, because he wasn't ruthless enough, or because he wasn't very good at fighting battles? Blood was nearly spilt on the bus when the lad with Scottish ancestry began crowing after we talked about Bannockburn. There was far more entertainment in all this than in the average episode of 'Eastenders'. The castle itself and its bleak location had not disappointed.

But now they were all silent.

A circuitous route into Norwich meant most of the young people could be dropped off along the way. Among them was Danny. Back at the unit I saw the remaining youngsters into their taxis and then went inside to telephone Danny's mum.

"Hello, Mrs Wright? It's Dom from Respect."

"Hello, Love."

"Had an issue today with Danny."

Having acknowledged and praised how well Danny had behaved and joined in the day's activities, I then described the incident on the way home that had spoiled his day.

"Oh sorry love. He gets it from his brothers I'm afraid. They've all been arrested for one thing or another, and the police are always around here making a nuisance of themselves. I'll have words with him."

"Thanks Mrs Wright. Will you let him know that we are going to have to talk about it tomorrow? And that he will have to write a letter of apology before he goes out with us again?"

Danny did really well with us. We got him back into school to take GCSEs, supported him in college applications and he went on to train as a chef. He'll probably have his own TV show eventually and become famous for his rudeness, bad language and bullying of his sous-chefs.

11 Susan

too tough a case

Danny was a simple case of a boy who needed structure in his life, firm discipline and boundaries, and as many opportunities to get it wrong and mess up as were needed without anyone giving up on him. There were many children like Danny, and we managed them easily. There were others that we found a lot more difficult and a few who were quite beyond our skills. We were familiar with children who had lower level mental disorders such as eating disorders or post-traumatic stress disorder arising from some adverse childhood experience. However, we were out of our depth when dealing with psychotic disorders such as severe bi-polarism or schizophrenia.

Despite this awareness of being unqualified, from time to time we still found ourselves having to cope with children who desperately needed therapy, but for whom, at that point in time, our service was all that was available. Probably, we should have refused to take such cases on, but often, when we agreed to get involved, the full nature of the problem wasn't apparent. It was very hard to turn a child away when we were told there was currently no treatment available and no alternative to our provision.

Susan's was this sort of case. Her story starts with an observation by Denise on a trip to the zoo.

The lioness had stopped her restless pacing the moment she saw Susan. Both remained rooted - staring into each other's eyes. The huge creature slowly settled onto her haunches, never taking her eyes off the girl. Susan mirrored her movements, sinking onto all fours and then back onto her heels, all the time looking deep into the cat's yellow brown eyes.

Unnoticed by either, Denise stood and watched from a distance across the enclosure. She had never seen Susan so quiet and calm. Something remarkable was happening. There was an electric tension between the two, both so still but with every sense sharpened, taut, like they might both leap towards each other at any moment. Denise wondered if Susan saw something in the lioness that perhaps mirrored her own existence. A restless energy now completely stilled? A sense of power ... of danger? All that majesty and power, at the very pinnacle of the food chain, yet trapped behind bars, prey to the whims of its captors? Was the big cat a kindred spirit who understood?

At our debriefing meeting that evening, Denise related this story of how Susan, crouched, still, quiet, had remained completely focused for about ten minutes. As so often happened at our meetings, Susan became the focus of conversation, with the staff reflecting yet again on the progress we were making – or not making - with her. Was this a new insight that would help us understand what made her tick?

With Liz, I had attended the meeting at which we'd agreed to take Susan on. It was in the neighbouring county, a school previously unknown to us, and our contact was an ex-colleague who had become a pastoral deputy head. We got the impression we'd been called in only because the school was desperate. They had made an attempt to exclude the girl and the county's children's services had objected very strongly! At the meeting, as well as the girl's case worker, there was a rarely seen educational psychologist and a high ranking official of the authority. The school and its deputy head were clearly under scrutiny.

At that meeting we were told nothing about Susan's background, just that she constantly took terrible risks and from the school's point of view was uncontrollable, a liability to herself and the staff responsible for her. She was said to be a danger to other pupils, always a red light in discussions. It was clear that, from the local authority's point of view, she was on a journey to a 'more appropriate' long term care and educational provision but nothing suitable was currently available. Respect4us was a stop-gap solution. It was hoped we could help her find a safe, calm place to be in her life until such time as therapeutic support was found.

To begin with, we actually thought Susan might be an asset to our centre. She appeared open, talkative, outgoing, sociable, inquisitive. But it didn't take long for it to become clear that she was deaf to any instruction she didn't want to hear. She had her own agenda and nothing would distract her from it. She had no interest in making friends with girls because her agenda was mainly about sex. She would hang around the older boys, insisting on being the centre of their attention and would do the same with male members of staff. We quickly realised that all male staff needed a chaperone when with Susan, for their own protection.

Susan would push us as far as she could and cause mischief wherever possible. Occasional glimpses however would reveal, under the wild child act and hard exterior, feelings of confusion, desperation and anger. She was, in essence, when all was stripped away, a small child desperate to be loved. But her walls were thick and strong, and very rarely did she let her guard down to reveal the vulnerability underneath. Predictably, whenever this happened, Susan would up her game and there would be another bout of provocative behaviour designed to elicit a reaction. Staff would ignore as much of this as possible and balance it with positive comments and de-escalation tactics. No one found it easy but we managed to cope, working as a team and mutually supporting one another. When one member of staff was tired of working with Susan another would take over. We looked for all the positives we could.

We were making progress, however slow. But then the vagaries of 'the system' kicked in, and all our carefully planned work to build relationships and a sense of self for Susan, disappeared overnight. The out-of-county taxi suddenly stopped coming. Our enquiries revealed that Children's Services were aware of the situation, but we were told no more. We could only assume that things had moved forward towards provision of the care that Susan needed and that we wouldn't see her again. No-one let us know.

A few months later, however, we got a call from our own local authority Children's Services asking us to attend a case conference to discuss Susan. And of course we went. At the meeting we learned that Susan was now in a children's residential home in a different coastal town and on the roll of another high school. We never found out what had happened to her in the meantime. She seemed simply to have disappeared off everyone's radar, and perhaps everyone had just breathed a sigh of relief. She had told those now responsible for her that she had liked her time at Respect and wanted to come back. Before agreeing, we decided to meet with Susan to find out why she wanted to return and what she wanted to get out of working with us.

As so often happens in those meetings of maybe a dozen adults around a table, all talking their professional talk, the sole child among them stands out as intensely lonely, lost and vulnerable, and your heart goes out to them. We learned that her new residential home was struggling to manage her behaviour; she was running away, would accept lifts from any stranger and was frequently staying out all night. There was concern about her promiscuity and she was well known to the county police as a child at risk. The decision of the conference was that she needed to be in a secure unit but that there was no suitable placement currently available. The school had nothing for her and her care workers were at their wits' end. Would Respect be kind enough to take her on for the time being?

Of course we would because that's what we do.

To begin with things went well. Susan arrived everyday by taxi without fuss. She did not run away from the care home and her social worker began giving her more privileges. She got a part-time job in a cafe. At Respect she was generally compliant, worked well with adults and stayed away from the younger children in the Centre. We began to think we might be getting somewhere. It didn't last.

It is little things that build up the positive over time but it is also little things and far away decisions that can destroy it. The powers in charge of school transport decided to put two new Year 11 boys in the same taxi as Susan as they all lived reasonably close. Maybe a sensible economic decision but in terms of Susan's life and prospects a big mistake! It's a 45 minute ride from the coastal towns into the city. Susan was travelling unsupervised with two older boys. One could only pity the poor taxi driver! Whatever happened on the journey Susan was loud, uncooperative and aggressive when she arrived. The boys made it clear they did not want her around them. Yet another rejection for this much rejected and deeply damaged young woman.

From then on Susan seemed unreachable. It would often take all day and the full-time attention of at least one member of staff to keep her calm. There were frequent angry outbursts and she brought a level of chaos into proceedings that unsettled everyone. On several occasions we had to call the taxi company to take her home early. After one particularly horrendous morning where Susan had been abusive and violent towards staff and other children we knew that we had to get her away from the Centre. We telephoned the children's home but they had no one to come and collect her, so we said we would bring her home ourselves. We loaded her and the two Year 11 boys into a minibus for an 'outing to the coast'. Liz kept her distracted, as she does so brilliantly, by striking up interesting conversations. When we pulled up outside the care home Susan didn't immediately realise where she was and followed Liz calmly out of the bus.

Liz walked her to the driveway entrance.
"You're home Susan. Go on inside."
Susan seemed to wake from a trance.
"No!" she yelled. "I'm not going home." She turned back to the minibus.

Liz rang the doorbell and then followed Susan, signalling to me to lock the doors. A care worker appeared at the doorway but didn't come out to join us.

Having tried the passenger door and found it locked, Susan circled the bus. We let Liz in.

Watching in the rear view mirror I was pleased to see the two boys seated at the back had not moved an inch.

"Mad, in't she Liz", said one of them.

A hammering began on the side of the bus.

"Open the door Liz, you bitch!"

Liz got on her phone to the home. "Hi, it's Liz from Respect. We are outside on the street with Susan. Can you come down and escort her in, please?"

The deafening hammering suddenly stopped.

Susan spoke nicely, "Liz, please let me in."

Then she screamed, "Liz, you fucking cow, let me in!"

BANG, BANG, BANG, down the side of the bus to the rear doors.

"Trent, quick, unlock the door," said Susan in a loud stage whisper through the closed back window. Watching in the mirror I saw Trent shrug his shoulders. Liam sat stony-faced, looking forwards.

Good boys, I thought. Now where are those care workers?

BANG, BANG, BANG, down the offside of the bus to the driver's door.

"Dom, Liz is being a right bitch. Can you let me in?"

Keep looking forward. Make no eye contact.

Round the front of the bus, BANG, on the bonnet. She pulled the wing mirror back, and let it thud back into place. She got to the front passenger door.

"Denise, pretty please, open the door, I need to get in. I'll be good I promise."

BANG, BANG, BANG, on the window. She twisted and yanked on the wing mirror.

Liz announced, "They are not going to come out. I am sorry but we are just going to have to leave her. Can you drive off, Dom?"

I started the engine, put it into gear, checked the mirrors. Was Susan clear of the bus? The nearside wing mirror was now uselessly pointing down at the road.

I asked Denise to straighten the mirror. This was a mistake. She cautiously began to wind the window down. As soon as there was a narrow gap Susan's hand was inside flailing at Denise's face. Denise rewound the window, gently pinching Susan's wrist. The flailing stopped and Denise released the pressure, the hand withdrew and the window shut fast.

All is quiet, can I move off? I thought.

"Is she clear of the side?" I asked.

Liz got up to check while I looked in the rear-view mirror. There was Susan, her face against the back widow, arms splayed across the back of the bus, like something from a horror film,

"She's standing on the rear step", I said, "I can't move off."

"Denise", said Liz, "We are going to have to get out. Lock the doors after us, Dom, and drive off as soon as we have got her clear. Stop somewhere away from here and I'll call you."

As soon as I saw Susan on the pavement with Liz and Denise each side of her, I pulled away and accelerated rapidly up the road.

Parking the minibus up on the clifftop I checked that Trent and Liam were OK. They'd found Susan amusing at first when they'd met her but had quickly grown tired of her antics. She wouldn't leave them alone and was quite explicit about what she wanted - didn't care much which of them it was! They were both sexually experienced enough to know that she was big trouble, as well as being only 14. Now they were sitting quietly waiting to see how the drama was going to unfold.

Left standing on the pavement with Susan, Liz and Denise told her to go home. Arms folded, she didn't move. When the two adults began to walk off she stuck to them. They rang the children's home for help and were told to call the police.

"Us coming out will make no difference. She won't do what we tell her. Call the police, it's their job."

You can feel very silly calling for a police officer because a child won't do as they're told and go home! So they carried on walking, hoping that Susan would give up. Down in the town they sat down on the steps of the fire station and tried to reason with her. But Susan was deaf to all persuasion. Liz had all the skills resulting from years of working with all sorts of difficult young people, and now to be unable to cope with being followed by a confused, frustrated and very vulnerable young person, one really no different to a screaming toddler, was not only challenging but frustrating – even humiliating.

Liz decided she had no choice – she phoned the police.
"Yes, we know all about Susan. We'll send a car."
The police car pulled up. The officer said from the window, "Get in Susan."
And she did. Just like that!

We didn't see Susan again.

At the end of the day, as we reflected on what had happened, we thought about what we might have done differently. Obviously, we knew we'd handled that day pretty badly, but sometimes you have to recognise that whatever you do it's not going to turn out well. Certainly, we felt we should have been able to expect better support from Susan's care workers.

So did Respect have any impact at all? We would like to think we got closer to Susan than any other educational provision. After all, she did like coming. But Susan's extreme behaviour was beyond our skills. Too much damage had already been done and probably at a very early age. Our reluctant conclusion was that we couldn't do any more for Susan and that, if she stayed with us, she would be a danger to others and to herself. All our skills had been exhausted. It was the first time we had given up on a child and we all felt very sad. Susan needed some form of on-going therapeutic help and we had to hope that eventually she received it.

We think we all learned from the experience of working with Susan. She was the most difficult case we had taken on so far. We had failed but I was really pleased that far from making us aware of our limitations and becoming more cautious about taking on tough cases, it had the opposite effect. It challenged us to up our game and we continued to welcome being given the cases everyone else considered hopeless. The fact that no two cases were ever the same made the job endlessly interesting. We had no one else exactly like Susan, but we had many more cases that were very demanding and we never gave up on any of them.

12 Jack

family and punishment

The normal lot of the teenager is to kick against the claustrophobic clutches of their family and parents. This is a perfectly normal part of growing up. Teenagers can't be expected to appreciate the value of what they have. Its value is perhaps only clear to the children who lack any kind of family love and support. Without this firm base it's not surprising children find it difficult to go out into the world, engage with school, with work, form relationships and have successful lives.

This was the issue Jack had. He never talked about his family so it took us a while to work out what his trouble was. Gradually, Respect4us became his family and like normal teenagers he kicked against the traces to see what he could get away with, to test us out. Would we continue to love him? Like all parents we had to decide how we were going to react to this testing. This chapter includes some discussion of our approach to punishment.

Jack was in local authority care and just wanted to be with his mum. This was the one thing that was not allowed to him. We never knew why. Like so many of our young people we knew very little about him. Whatever had gone on before, we promised kids a fresh start, a blank record sheet. We would accept each new child as we found them. Of course from a safeguarding point of view there were certain things we just had to know. With Jack, we knew that he was in care, that he didn't get on in school and that on no account was he to be allowed to make contact with his mum.

Jack was delightful, very direct, and said exactly what was on his mind, but usually in a way that was polite and inoffensive. He could be very funny. We guessed that he was somewhere on the autistic spectrum, and certainly the other kids found him strange, generally giving him a wide berth. He didn't seem to care and had little interest in making friends with his peers. Mostly he wanted to be with the adults; he would sit in on informal staff meetings and take part in the chit-chat. His catchphrase was, "I tell you what.." which littered his conversation and which he would repeat if he felt he didn't have enough of your attention. It was like talking to an old guy in a pub, "I tell you what, mate....." and who would then proceed to give you some dogmatically held opinion.

Jack would usually have a strong favourite whom he would follow around with a constant stream of talk. For a while it was me but then he latched onto Joseph. Joseph came to us originally as a temporary, part-time member of staff while he was still at university. He was young, super fit, and great at all types of sport. We took on a lot of youngsters as staff because they had the energy vital for an organisation aiming to physically exhaust its clients. If they had a bit of personality and a bit of steel in them we knew they were probably going to be good at the work. They were also likely to be more in tune with our youngsters than older people like me and Liz. Our job was to provide the leadership, the training, the advice and guidance they needed.

Joseph was outstanding, showing real aptitude for the work. After completing his degree he stayed on with us and had a permanent job, eventually becoming a unit manager. When he finally left us it was to become a qualified teacher. He now runs a PE department in a large secondary school.

It was Joseph who started table tennis. One day he brought in a sheet of eight by four ply, and he, Jason and a group of young people taped markings on it, got themselves a net, table tennis bats and ping-pong balls and set it up across tables in the workshop. It was hours of fun and a huge success. There were ping-pong balls everywhere and they were constantly being found in the nooks and crannies of the workshop. We were all so pleased to get young people away from their screens and video games. It was a godsend on wet days when getting out for activity was difficult. Along with the pool table, table tennis would keep teenagers occupied for hours. It wasn't just fun; there were many skill outcomes. As well as the physical skills, the brain, hand, eye coordination, they learned to lose gracefully, or to win and not crow about it too much; learning to react to triumph and disaster with the same aplomb.

There was a constant queue to play and of course champions began to emerge. The aim of all new and upstart players was to topple a champion and Joseph was the champion of champions. He was a very young member of staff and the idea of allowing a young person to beat him - which many of the more experienced staff members would do - was complete anathema to him. Now Jack got it into his head that he had to beat Joseph. It became a total obsession that he never gave up on no matter how many times he was beaten.

"I tell you what Joseph, I am going to beat you today."

"I tell you what Joseph, didn't I beat you yesterday?"

"I tell you what Joseph, I am so much better at table tennis than you."

This banter would go on for hours.

For Jack, we became the family that was so missing in his everyday life. He didn't talk about his mum or anyone else in his family. We knew nothing about that side of his life or even if there was any family apart from mum, but we knew mum was never far from his thoughts.

One day Donna's phone went missing. It had been in her jacket which she hung on the coat hooks in the training room. She only realised it was missing when she got home from work and her daughter told her she had been getting strange texts from her phone. It didn't take her long to realise someone from work must have it and with the messages on her daughter's phone she guessed it was Jack.

Jack was refusing to come into Respect the next morning, so Donna and Liz arranged to go out to his residential home to talk to him. Jack wouldn't come out of his room but one of the care workers had already retrieved the phone from him. She explained to Liz why she thought Jack had taken it. He would talk to his mum on the phone every night but this was always on an official phone, for a short fixed period of time and with a care worker present to monitor what they talked about. Jack complained constantly about this and was obsessed with being able to talk to his mum on his own. This was why he had taken the phone. He had only used it to talk to his mum and to send text messages to Donna's daughter who had worked with us for a while so he knew her and had liked her.

Liz sat outside Jack's bedroom and talked to him through the closed door. She discovered eventually that he was terrified Respect wouldn't allow him to come back because of what he'd done. After much reassurance, he emerged from the bedroom and apologised to Donna. He said he had thought he could just borrow the phone and return it the next day and that we wouldn't mind. He realised now he'd made a big mistake.

Donna was not happy with the apology and thought there should be very serious consequences for theft. Liz listened sympathetically but held her ground. One of our core beliefs in setting up Respect was that punishment doesn't work. It just further alienates children who are already disaffected. For children with learning difficulties or who have been through trauma, the connection between cause and effect is not always obvious. Human societies and adult behaviour can be full of inconsistencies and hypocrisy and young people are quite adept at identifying these. 'Do as I say and not as I do,' is an approach taken by many adults to managing children's behaviour. But if we are serious about changing children's behaviour it is vitally important for us to consistently model the behaviour we expect.

Unfortunately, the belief that punishment works runs deep in our society. As a result of the pressure we put on weak politicians, we lock up a higher proportion of our population than any country in Europe; and without there being any impact on crime levels. The sad fact is that it's largely the same group of people who are on the prison merry-go-round, constantly in and out of prison throughout their lives. The proportion who go to prison once, learn their lesson and then go straight is tiny. The children we worked with - the broken, the damaged, those in gangs, those involved with serious drugs, those with special needs and disabilities - all of them would become the adults who would normally end up in the prisons. We believed we could break this vicious cycle and prevent the massive cost to society in wasted lives, victim damage and the eye-watering financial cost of the criminal justice system. Politicians please note that Respect4us was working on this day-in, day-out, and doing it on a shoestring budget!

So what was the solution? What did we do to turn these children around, to get them off the conveyor belt to crime, prison and a wrecked life? There was no one simple answer but always basic principles that were followed - the principles of good parenting. Children needed to be listened to, and a real effort made to get to the heart of what was troubling them. The adults had to demonstrate that they were not going to give up, that they could be trusted always to do what was best for the child. A few children were too damaged, too far gone to be reached, but for most there was an approach that could make a difference. It's extraordinarily difficult work because many of these kids made themselves very difficult to like. You need patience, resilience and self-belief to withstand the constant battering they could give you.

In the end we agreed that Jack would be prevented from going on our trip to the County Show later in the week, and that was a big disappointment for him. It was a punishment for him that he took seriously. He'd made a mistake which had a consequence but we made sure the mistake had absolutely no impact on his relationships.

Jack was a success story. Respect gave him what he craved most - an experience of family. He was liked, he was trusted, he was wanted and he was loved. Of course he couldn't stay at Respect for ever but he learned that there could be other people out there apart from his mum who could love him. We never did discover what the issue was with his mum.

13 David

bikes across Norfolk

Much of my time (when I wasn't working with young people) was spent worrying about how Respect was to be funded. It was a hand-to-mouth existence and I could never be certain there would be enough to pay wages and bills the following month. As the government policy of "Austerity" bit harder, we knew schools had more and more difficulty finding funds to pay us. We just survived by keeping our costs to a minimum and our staff, including directors, on minimum wage. We approached all the local businesses in the neighbourhood and then in the city for help with the extras we wanted to provide but little was forthcoming. One representative of a wonderful organisation that did support us, summed up our problem:

"You do know, you're never going to be on TV?" said Julie, the BBC lady, "like, I mean, televised for showing on 'Children in Need'. I'm afraid your kids just aren't fluffy and cuddly at all, are they?"

"I agree, of course," I replied. "Most people won't put their hands in their pockets if they think their money is going to undeserving teenage layabouts." I laughed, "Some people are very vocal about that!"

"Nonetheless," Julie added supportively, "don't tell anyone, but you are exactly the sort of organisation we do want to help at Children in Need. We just won't be advertising it to the general public."

BBC Children in Need supported us for a number of projects (as did the National Lottery). On this occasion we were seeking a grant to help pay for a residential experience involving a night away in a hostel. Our young people were going to get to the hostel by bike and we needed a bike trailer which Children in Need paid for, and they paid for the hire of the hostel. We had already had help from Norfolk Police who provided us with bikes.

David's story starts as we were taking receipt of a load of bikes that had come from a police warehouse.

David once more sauntered nonchalantly around the van. He glanced through the open front window. He could see the key was in the ignition. He leaned on the bonnet as though in deep thought and looked back towards Liz. He satisfied himself that she was fully engaged in conversation with the policeman. She just never stops talking, he thought. He hated coppers. The disgusting sleaze-bag was just chatting her up - and she's old enough to be his nan, he thought.

He slid along the front of the van, keeping half an eye on the two adults. They were still talking. Now or never, he thought. He opened the passenger door a crack, just wide enough to squeeze in. He pulled himself up and shut the door as gently as quietly as he could. He slithered across to the driver's seat, adjusting it as far forward as it would go. He could just reach the pedals. Check the gears. Turn on the ignition.

At that moment a hand shot through the window and attached itself firmly to the key before he could reach it.
"David Winters, out you get!"
"Awh, Liz…"
"I've got eyes in the back of my head, you know. I always know exactly what you're up to."
She held the door open and David climbed reluctantly down.
"Now, get inside and sit down with Denise. I want that English work done. I'll speak to you in a minute."
David shuffled off towards the unit, muttering under his breath, "..'kin miserable cow."
Liz turned back to the young police officer who was now slightly red-faced.
"Not a clever move around here leaving the keys in. But thanks for the bikes."
"Yeh, well… sorry. Ok then, I'd better be off. Let us know if you want any more. We've always got loads more in the warehouse."
He got into the driver's seat, pushing it back as he went.

"You know, I don't know how you work with kids like that all day."
"What? My little Davie? But he's a little sweetie!"

David was the scrawniest under-sized thirteen year old I had ever come across. He was incredibly cheeky and utterly brazen in his lying, cheating and thieving! He was a lovable rogue straight out of a Dickens novel - or, as Liz put it, "a little sweetie". We had already come across one of David's older brothers. Stan had attended Respect the year before and we had parted from him on rather unhappy terms. He had sat down to talk to Liz at the end of a day - an unusual occurrence as he was not particularly talkative and we felt we had not yet won his trust. During their talk she was distracted for a few moments and then she realised Stan had gone. A minute or two later she realised her phone had gone with him. We went round to his address and the door was answered by a scruffy and surly young man, whom we took to be an older brother, but who wouldn't give us his name. He denied that anyone called Stan had ever lived there and shut the door in our faces. Stan did not appear at Respect again.

With David we had made some headway and he had learned to trust us. Though we were never foolish enough to fully trust him, we all liked him. He was always so cheerful and playful, direct, disrespectful, irrepressible! His home life was chaotic with a host of older siblings who between them were probably responsible for a high proportion of the petty crime in Norwich. Mum was not in evidence at all. A lot of the time David used to live with his grandmother and when we met her we understood where his likeability came from. She was another "sweetie"! She was infirm and hardly ever went out of her flat. David was her main carer. They adored each other. But he couldn't always stay there as she was frequently in hospital. At one point David excitedly told us that dad had reappeared and asked David to go and live with him. It only lasted a week, just long enough for someone to come and assess dad's housing needs as a single parent. Once the inspection was over, dad's girlfriend moved back in and David was told to go back to mum or Nan, dad didn't care which. For a few days David lost his usual bounce.

David was involved in our bikes project from the start. He was one of several who were really into their BMX bikes. One of them even cycled regularly into the unit from a village seven or eight miles away. Quite a feat on a BMX! The kids with bikes were much in demand as everybody wanted to borrow them to practice their tricks or to race around the BMX track in the local park. We wondered if we were to get some proper mountain or road bikes we might expand their horizons by doing expeditions out on the many cycle tracks and byways that criss-crossed the Norfolk countryside. It would be a change from walking.

It had been Liz's idea to approach the police to see if they had any bikes we could have.

"Bikes? We've got a warehouse full of them. You can have as many as you want," was the reply, when she made tentative enquiries at the main city police station.

Apparently bikes are picked up by the police, abandoned all over the city, or they get to the warehouse as a result of raids to retrieve stolen goods and are never claimed by their owners. To be fair some of them were little better than scrap metal, but Jason felt that he could make at least a dozen of them roadworthy without any great expense. We had time, we had a willing labour force and we had a reasonably well-equipped workshop.

Jason got to work with a group of keen bike engineers. The police bikes were soon stripped down, repairs made and parts replaced. Another group had gone out to visit all the local bike shops to see if they could beg spare parts or at least get them at cost, but not one of them was so generous. There was virtually no money for the project so Jason made do by cannibalising parts from the bikes that were beyond repair. One result of this was that when we did eventually get out biking we had constant breakdowns. Another problem was how to store all these bikes that were now cluttering up the unit. I had already begun work to solve these problems by applying for a grant from Children in Need. Having a bike trailer would mean we could store the bikes off site and could get out of the city quickly and easily to ride in the countryside. ⌐SEP⌐

Jason didn't mind fixing the bikes up but he was a reluctant cyclist. Nonetheless, he and Joseph did a course and got qualified to lead groups both on and off road. Biking became a popular activity. The bike laden trailer was now kept in a storage unit on another industrial estate and would be collected on the days we were going biking. First each bike would need to be checked over and repairs done. Another group would decide where we were going and plot routes. There were some favourite places that we would go back to again and again such as an area of woodland that we knew had plenty of hills and jumps. BMXing was still the favourite activity. Of course the bikes, always fairly delicate, took a terrible hammering. Sometimes we would go for distance, cycling out on the old railway trails and being picked up by the minibus and trailer miles down the route. When we thought the young people were ready we began planning a two day expedition and staying somewhere overnight. This was to be the first Respect4us residential.

Organising this was a lot more difficult than organising a school residential. For a start all the young people came to us through different schools and organisations so many more permissions needed to be sought. While some kids had been with us for a year or more, many were quite new to us and didn't yet have the level of trust. There was a huge range in needs and ages that had to be taken into account. A lot of planning was necessary and it took rather more selling to the young people than we had expected. One young person really wanted to do the ride but had big concerns about staying overnight and would need to be taken home. Jack wanted to go but couldn't bear the thought of missing his supervised phone call to his mum in the evening. Gradually permissions were sought and problems overcome. Everyone was included in the challenge though it was always clear that some would have to be brought back for the night in time for their various lifts and taxis.

Liz found a hostel in the west of Norfolk in a very isolated spot. Its location meant we could use an old railway line, the Marriott's Way, to get away from the city and then make the rest of the journey using bridleways and quiet country lanes. We would have exclusive use of the building - no one to upset! - and there were no near neighbours. The minibus (with trailer for broken down bikes) would meet the riders at various staging points. There would be refreshments and lunch of course, and an opportunity for riders to swap over, so anyone tired could do a leg in the minibus.

Everyone did some riding and everyone was enjoying themselves. There were the furious cyclists who steamed on ahead but were never allowed to go beyond the next minibus rendezvous; there were the gentle cyclists who pottered along enjoying the countryside; and in between there were the boys pulling their wheelies and doing jumps at every opportunity. The BMX fanatic stuck to his principles and only rode his BMX. Standing all the way on his pedals, he was exhausted by the end but it was his choice! When the time came in mid-afternoon for the returning group to leave many of them did not want to go.

The night at the hostel was a real adventure for most of them. We were miles from anywhere and so there were no distractions. There was no phone signal unless you were prepared to walk half a mile up the lane. For a while there was some bickering over sleeping space and who was in which room but pretty soon they all came to the conclusion that it was only one night and having their own space didn't matter at all. A lot of planning by the young people had gone into food and they all had their own jobs in preparing a meal. When this was out of the way and dusk was falling everybody was outside to listen for the owls and to spook each other in the gloom. For most it was a completely novel experience to be out in the stillness and dark of the countryside with no artificial light apart from the minimal amount coming from our own building. We had located the fire pit on arrival and were ready to light a fire and then have all the normal human campfire experiences from toasting marshmallows to telling ghost stories. When we eventually came inside none of the young people wanted to be apart during the night so they all moved their mattresses into the common room and the telling of stories went on long into the night.

This was an adventure none of these children would forget.

14 Ada

coping with adolescence

Not all children who came our way were in care or from troubled families. Some were just suffering the pain of adolescence more than most. Ada was one of these.

Liz was sitting in the kitchen catching up with paperwork when Vannessa interrupted:
"Sorry, Liz. I've got someone in the office to see you if you've got a minute. She's a parent... but not one of ours. I'm not sure... I think you need to talk to her. But I can say you are busy, if you like?"
"No, this report is driving me mad. Talking to anyone would be a relief. The forms we have to fill in these days just get more and more stupid!"
Pushing her chair back, Liz rose and followed Vannessa through the workshop to the office.
Sitting in front of Vannessa's desk was a youngish woman, maybe late thirties, smartly dressed in a business suit. Not the normal sort of parent we see in here, thought Liz.
"Hello, I'm Liz. What can I...."
"I want a place here for my daughter," interrupted the woman brusquely.
"OK, but that's not quite how we do things here," responded Liz, easing herself into Vannessa's desk seat. "Let's start with introductions and then you can tell me all about it. I'm Liz Easton, managing director of Respect4us. Clearly you know something about Respect4us already or you wouldn't be here. But who are you?"
"I'm Debbie Virtanen. Finnish name... my husband's.... ex-husband's name....I've kept it because I like his mum ... out of respect for his mum. Ada is his daughter... our daughter ... and it's her I'm here about. I've done my research and I want her to come here."
"OK...," said Liz, guardedly. "How old is Ada, Mrs Virtanen?"
"Debbie... please. She's fifteen."

"So, isn't she in school?"

"Oh, yes. Officially yes. But she's not going anymore. It's anxiety. She has panic attacks. She just can't cope with school. She was fine in primary school but at high school she's just found it more and more difficult and especially after her dad and I broke up."

"OK Debbie, she sounds like the sort of child we can work with but we can't just take children here because they want to come to us or because their parents want them to come to us. We are not a school and every child has to be on the roll of a school. So in Ada's case it means she still has to belong to a school and that school has to want her to come to us...... unless of course you are officially homeschooling...?"

"No, she's still on roll at school. But don't worry about them. I'll deal with them," she said confidently. "But could she have a place here?"

"Well, we'd have to meet her first of course, and the school would have to officially ask us to take her... and agree to pay for her place here..."

"Oh, don't worry about that," interrupted Debbie. "I know what you do here and it's what I want for Ada. So we'll pay....or her father will."

Clearly Mrs Virtanen was a woman of some clout because the next morning a deputy head from Ada's school was on the phone. She sounded harassed as though she had been given a hard time and said she had to come and talk to us urgently. She appeared in person later in the morning together with Ada's head of year and the school's special educational needs co-ordinator. They clearly had a high opinion of Ada and her academic potential but were honest about how they were now at a complete loss as to how to move her forward. They had tried everything they could think of to settle her and had explored every avenue to get to the bottom of what was causing the anxiety. All they could do now was suggest to mum that Ada worked at home with on-line support for the rest of her final year at school. It was this suggestion that had led Mrs Virtanen to seek out Respect4us.

95

The school was not one that had worked with us before so understandably the teachers were there to check us out. Having had the tour and the talk they seemed satisfied and were even prepared to pay for the maximum three days a week. On the remaining two days Ada would work at home and receive on-line teaching support in her core subjects.

Getting to know Ada was a delight and not what we expected at all. Her anxiety levels were off the scale but there was nothing timid, shy or retiring about her. The first thing you noticed about her were her outrageously long, false eyelashes. In virtually any high school this alone would get a student into trouble but the teachers hadn't mentioned it. Clearly the eye lashes were a vitally important part of her self-image. She was constantly having to attend to them and re-fix them with glue. The first thing we did, after admiring them and saying how cool they were, was to make sure we had a spare set of eyelashes on the premises along with plenty of glue.

And then she was loud! To the average person on the street she would have come across as loudly and unattractively foul-mouthed. Underneath, for anyone who had the patience and took the trouble to look, was a very scarred, but kind and caring young person. This person underneath was hard to find because Ada was quite determined not to let anyone in, and the image that was all-important to her, would be protected whatever the cost.

Such a complex character! She would come in after a weekend and her personality would fill the building, leaving no room for anyone else. For a while everyone would hear all about her weekend, an account that would include every sordid detail of what she and her mates had got up to, and probably a few things they hadn't done but had fantasised about. Adults could be aghast and appalled, the more mature young people cynical - "Whatever, Ada...," - and the more easily impressed, admiring. It was all an act!

On other occasions she could be found behind the unit crying her eyes out and she would be taken into the office for a heart to

96

heart. These were not very productive to begin with. Ada would find her composure, sort her eyelashes out, and put on her hard as nails skin once more. But bit by bit over the weeks she learned to trust and to realise that she could talk in confidence, treating the staff as sounding boards to help her vocalise and begin to make some sense of her feelings.

She loved her mum but they drove each other mad and argued constantly. Her Nana was her rock and she would often go to stay with her when things got particularly bad at her mum's. Nana was her release valve. She was endlessly patient, non-judgemental and not in the slightest threatened by Ada. We would have liked to have given Nana a job! Unfortunately she spent a lot of time back in Finland and when she was away we knew there would be trouble with Ada. At these times Ada learned to use Liz as her Nana, - to the great amusement of the rest of us! That role was not a comfortable one as Liz found she would get the full tempestuous blast of Ada's anger and frustration. Liz also had to learn a certain amount of Finnish as this was how Ada liked to talk to her Nana!

Ada loved her dad and had a room at his house but staying with dad was no escape capsule. Dad did not have his mother's patience. To make matters worse Ada could not stand her stepmother. Whenever she was at her dad's she would come to Respect in a foul temper. We would hear all about it, and even after making allowances for her bias, it was clear that dad and stepmum did not have a clue about managing teenage behaviour. The way Ada told the story of her time with them it usually sounded as though she herself had been the adult in the room.

Ada was on medication for ADHD. We do not presume to be health experts or pretend to have any kind of medical qualification but with Ada, as with so many other children, we did wonder whether the medication was warranted. Ada hated taking it and we didn't make an issue of that. Most days we set out to exhaust her instead. She loved all types of sport and she was incredibly competitive. Whatever physical activity we were doing she would always want to be the best - and would delight in being able to beat both Paul and Levi. She had great stamina, was particularly good at running and had been trained to do gymnastics to a high level. She was also very bright and given her background had had experiences and knowledge shared by few of our other students. She would frequently initiate and lead discussions.

Ada was indeed a complex character, one with loads of positives: a huge personality, a great big heart, a fabulous sense of humour, a keen intelligence, a determination to succeed; but alongside all those qualities was a ferocious temper and an impulse to self-destruct that could terrify all around her. She had ups and downs that were among the most extreme we had ever seen. Over the years she had built up a shield wall to protect herself but under that was a gentle and thoughtful kindness. Perhaps the most unique thing of all was her ability to completely disarm you by apologising with absolute sincerity.

Later in the year she fell in love. Predictably it was with absolutely the wrong guy. She was used and lied to but couldn't see it for herself. We heard all about it from her and we also heard the great concerns of both her mum and her school. We talked with the school to make sure we were all satisfied it was not a safeguarding issue. Mum had already tried to forbid the liaison - a line that was never going to work with Ada! - the school agreed with us that Ada had to be in control of her own life and the relationship would run its own course. When the fallout came, for Ada, it was the end of the world. She took it very hard and we all had to patiently support her while she gradually pieced her life back together.

We created an individual cocoon for her away from the normal group activities and used the space to get her to start focusing on her own future - leaving school was now only months away. She decided she wanted to do a childcare course at college and we began to put together a functional skills course that would get her to where she needed to be. To begin with in her fragile state she only wanted to be with Liz and would work with her in the office. We knew she was making progress when she announced that Liz's maths skills were rubbish and she would need a different tutor. Tony took over and became her mentor in the weeks that followed.

When exams week arrived, everyone was concerned that Ada wouldn't turn up or would refuse to do them. She surprised us all by taking them very seriously and observing exam conditions throughout. Of course she passed and then we were looking seriously at college applications.

An interview was arranged. Ada panicked and said she wouldn't go. A new round of coaching began before finally she agreed to go as long as Liz accompanied her. On the day of the interview they went by public transport using the route that Ada would need to take when she went on her own from home. They explored the college, had coffee, and got used to the new environment before heading off for the interview together. We had already briefed the college about Ada and they got things exactly right. The interviewer was relaxed and friendly, and gradually coaxed Ada into talking about herself. She was offered a place. She had a future.

Most children sail through childhood and the whole awkward process of growing up. For some it just all goes wrong and they lose their way. Compared with many, Ada had so much going for her. She had a family that got many things completely wrong, but they loved her and were totally committed to her. The family was far more affluent than most we saw at Respect. Ada had never wanted for anything in life. In particular she had a mother who would fight tooth and nail for her daughter. If her mother had not looked into alternative provision and discovered Respect4us, Ada might well have drifted off to join so many others in drugs and crime on the fringes of society. She also benefited from having a school that would go the extra mile to meet her needs.

We never got to the bottom of what caused her anxiety but believed in the end it didn't really matter. Ada just needed time and patience and support to get her through adolescence.

Respect4us took all the pressure away. What we gave her was unconditional support.

15 Pete, George, Harry (1)
driving motivation

Liz peered into the distance. The runway seemed to stretch out into the distance, dropping below the curvature of the Earth and into infinity. There was a shimmering midday haze that obscured the view. Where were they? Perhaps this had not been such a good idea.

"What's happened to them?" she said aloud.

"Stop worrying, Liz!" said Vanessa B, firmly.

Vanesa was sitting beside Liz, behind the steering wheel of her open-topped mini which was on the apron of one of the many airfields that still littered the East Anglian countryside.

"There's nothing to worry about," repeated Vanessa. "Martin is a fantastic instructor and is obsessive about safety. Driving up there they couldn't have been doing more than twenty. Even with an idiot like Pete at the wheel, they are not going to come to any harm. Look, there they are!"

Liz scanned the horizon, wishing she hadn't left her glasses at home. In the haze she thought she could see a tiny black dot. The dot became a car alarmingly quickly. The Audi was suddenly right in front of them. She realised Vanessa was cheering excitedly and waving her arms above her head. Liz could hardly bear to look.

"Oh my god, they must be doing 120!" she whispered, appalled, slumping deeper into her seat.

The Audi was slowing now. Towards the end of the runway it circled and then came slowly back to join them on the apron. Harry jumped out of the back and pulled the driver's door open.

"Amazing!' said Pete, still clinging to the steering wheel, "Did you see me Liz?"

"My turn! Get out!" said Harry.

"Calm down, young man, or we're not going anywhere," came the clear, firm voice of Martin, the driving instructor.

Pete unclipped his belt and climbed out.

"That's so cool. That's just brilliant, man." He talked excitedly at Liz and Vanessa as Harry climbed into the driving seat and Martin began again his slow explanation of the controls.

When this was complete, and he was certain that Harry had the hang of the gear movements, and could differentiate each of the pedals with his feet, he allowed him to re-start the engine. Pete joined George on the back seat.

"Now take your time," said Martin. "Depress the clutch. Find first gear. That's right. Release the handbrake. Slowly let the pedal come up. Find biting point. Right foot. A few revs."

The engine stalled. Pete jeered.

"Be quiet Pete! You did that too. Everyone does when they start driving. OK Harry, try again. Check you are out of gear before starting up."

After one more false start, the Audi moved off jerkily and headed slowly up the runway.

It had been Vanessa B's idea. Vanessa was a Respect 'patron'. She had heard about what we were doing and telephoned one day to volunteer support and help . When all the required checks on her were done she had become a frequent visitor and would help out where she could. Her idea had been to raise aspirations by laying on a driving experience. She argued that giving them a taste of what it was like to drive a good car would help them to understand why it was important to work hard, to sacrifice pleasures today so that you could have nice things tomorrow. Working hard to get a driving licence and a car could open new doors in their lives, both socially and in the choice of jobs they could do. She felt this was one of the biggest differences between these young people and those who were more successful in school. Liz thought it was a bit simplistic and certainly not the whole story but recognised that there was an element of truth in it. So Vanessa was allowed to go ahead and organise the driving experience day.

The experience had been offered to the three oldest boys who would all be leaving school at the end of the year. The driving instructor Vanessa found had a great reputation and quickly grasped what she was trying to achieve. He volunteered his services because he wanted to share his love of cars and because he recognised the importance of reaching potential tearaway drivers, and showing them how things could be done safely, while still having fun with cars. When he turned up in a brand new Audi the boys were really impressed. The location was the airfield used by the local gliding club. John, its commodore, was an ex-headteacher and since retirement had worked from time to time at Respect.

The day had gone really well. Martin spoke to them about the joy of driving, stressing all the time the importance of safety on the roads. He talked about how being able to drive gave people independence and freedom, opening up opportunities in life. It was also a necessary tool for very many jobs. The boys listened hard and soaked it all up.

Then it was on to the basics and they each had a turn behind the wheel. After lunch they were driving at speed with Vanessa cheering them on while Liz sat, nervously, feeling her hair go grey. But even Liz had to admit at the end of the day that it had been a success. The boys all thanked Martin very sincerely and shook his hand. He wished them luck with their futures and, of course, suggested they return to him for their driving lessons.

The success of the day was confirmed by the talk in Liz's car as she drove them home. She had expected them to talk solely about how fast they had gone but this figured little in the discussion. It was Harry who began talking about how stupid he thought his mates were now as they did completely reckless things on the road and when he could drive he wouldn't be doing anything like that. George agreed. He said he'd loved driving fast on the airfield but could see how stupid that would be on an ordinary road. They chatted about everything Martin had taught them, and about how they were going to get jobs so they could start saving for their provisional driving licences and future lessons.

Before leaving they thanked Liz for allowing them to do it.
"Best day ever at Respect," said Pete.
No one argued.
"Result," thought Liz, "and now home to get my hair dyed!"

16 Pete, George, Harry (2)
parenting failures

The three boys taken driving were all in Year 11 and about to leave school. All had responded brilliantly to the driving day. The driving instructor was really impressed with them and couldn't understand why they were with us and not in a school preparing for GCSEs.

Pete was one of several children but he was a lot younger than his brothers. He lived with his dad and stepmother. He would bounce around Tigger-like, full of enthusiasm for a project one moment, only to lose all interest the next. He was bubbly, friendly and personable but so very irritating. He would have been a perfectly normal teenager if only he had got the attention he needed at home. Stepmum was a much bigger presence in his life than his dad. She demanded a great deal of Pete and felt she had to be as strict as possible with him. He was clearly a mystery to her and of course he always fell below her expectations; which she let him know all about. She would tell anyone who listened about his misdeeds and about how useless he was. We realised that if anything at all critical was said to Pete, the shutters would come down, his ears would be closed, and his attention immediately would shift on to something else. We were sure this was learned behaviour from his relationship with stepmum.

Despite getting it all wrong his stepmum did at least care enough to want to help Pete. Inevitably, it was attention from his dad that Pete craved. When he wasn't working, his dad went fishing. Pete talked non-stop about fishing and it was always what he wanted to do when given the choice. However, when we did take him fishing, it was clear that he had no patience for it. He would bounce around on the river bank, ignoring his fishing tackle, upsetting those who were fishing seriously, and constantly looking for distractions. The obsession with fishing was all about wanting time with dad. He had been fishing with dad in the past but had clearly ruined his dad's fun and been banned from going again.

104

The result of this was a very emotionally vulnerable young man who was confused, angry, desperate to be loved and wanted, but let down by the adults in his life. He tried to get what he needed from his peers and was very easily led - frequently into trouble. Every incident in school, his eventual exclusion, increasing trouble with the police, all justified his dad in washing his hands of him, and his stepmum's nagging disappointment in him. Sometimes he would come to Respect in the morning seemingly completely happy and cheerful and then within minutes, with a murderous look on his face, be punching holes in doors.

The strategy we adopted involved endless patience and listening. All of us had to work at not letting his irritating behaviour get to us, especially the frustration of being blanked out by him. Wherever possible we would avoid reprimanding or criticising him. When things went wrong and he would drop a task in frustration, we would give him the space to move off to something else, but encouraged and supported him if he decided to come back to try again. Always we stressed that he was a learner and as such was expected to fail. We were here for him, he was not a disappointment, and definitely not a failure.

The other part of the strategy was to work with stepmum. It was she, we decided, who was the key person in Pete's life. If he was going to get any support at home it would be from her. We made contact with her and at every opportunity reported his successes. We made a point of only ever telephoning with good news. Little by little we began to coach her in how to get better results out of her stepson.

Sadly, a few weeks after the driving lesson Pete was taken into care and stopped attending Respect4us. A couple of years later Denise was in the city when she bumped into him. In fact he bounded up to her in characteristic Tigger style and gave her a hug. That's how we learned that he had gone to college after Year 11 and was now in employment and living an independent life.

As a character, George was totally different, but like Pete, he suffered from poor parenting, though of a very different order. George was unusual at Respect in very many ways. He was always immaculately turned out, well-groomed and coiffured, wearing expensive, labelled clothes. He stood out from the crowd. He was tall, good looking and oozed style. He rarely lost his temper or appeared frustrated. He spoke quietly and was polite. He had aspirations. He wanted to go to college and get a good job. So what was he doing at Respect?

He had come to us halfway through Year 11 after he had been excluded from school. Admittedly, the school was one with a very strict discipline code, and one that prided itself on having among the best results in the county. Nonetheless, to get thrown out in the final year of school would take quite a lot of determination on the part of a student, especially one as self-controlled as George. So what had happened?

We spent a lot of time as a team discussing things like this and didn't have a lot to go on apart from our observations of the way the young person behaved. Sometimes we would hear a very one-sided account of a personal history, but mostly youngsters had moved on by the time they got to Respect and wanted to forget about their past lives. We felt we needed to concentrate on how we were going to move each individual forward into a newly invented future. But if, as in George's case, there was little time left to collect new data, we relied on the past history to help us come to a rapid conclusion about the best strategy to adopt.

The picture that began to emerge of George was of a boy who had always had everything he wanted in the way of material things. Perhaps, in old-fashioned parlance, he was spoiled. His parents both had good jobs and there was no shortage of money. They seemed to have high aspirations for themselves, and probably for George, but they had little time for him. Having provided for him materially, they expected him to respond by being successful in school, sailing through exams, going on to college and a well-paid job. But underneath the suave exterior George lacked all confidence in himself. Did the pressure get too much for him? Did he panic and deliberately, or perhaps unconsciously, push the boundaries at school to the point of exclusion? Was it to avoid being found out by the exams and failing? Was it to get attention from his parents and the emotional support he needed?

Our strategy with George was to provide the close personal attention and emotional support that perhaps had been missing in his life. We stressed how much we believed in him and gave him endless encouragement. We worked closely with him on his college application, and gave him belief that he could get an academic career back on track. We helped him write personal statements that got across his strengths and determination to succeed. We did endless practice interviews. We reported back to his mother regularly to convince her that what had happened was no catastrophe, that lots of people messed up in school and that George was going to go to college; he just needed all around him to support him and to believe in him.

His mother accompanied George to his interview. She was the first to congratulate him when he was offered a college place.

Harry also had a comfortable background. He lived with mum in a nice home in a nice area. Mum was on her own with two children - there was a younger sister who was doing well in mainstream school. Mum cared deeply about Harry but was frequently at her wits' end as a working mum trying to fit everything in.

Harry came across as always grumpy with a sour face that made him difficult to be around. To begin with no one would ever get a smile or thank you from Harry; nothing was ever right; he was always negative. We had to dig very deep to get to know him, but those of us who managed to get under his armour discovered a rather sad and angry little boy. To his one or two confidantes among the staff, he eventually revealed how much he missed his dad. Mum had chucked dad out, and Harry knew in his heart that she was right to do so, but he still desperately missed him. At the confused age of fourteen it is so hard to make sense of these feelings. With no guidance from home - and perhaps lacking a male role model - Harry had got in with a crowd who led him into trouble - trouble with the law and trouble at school. By the time he came to us he was seriously depressed.

Following weekends spent with dad, Harry would often be in a worse mood than ever. Dad was a drinker. He managed to hold down a job but he was otherwise totally unreliable. Gradually over the course of a Monday, we would discover that Harry had spent virtually the entire weekend on his own, watching videos and playing video games, while dad had been in the pub.

We gave Harry space to be quiet on his own or gave him attention if he seemed to want it. He was put under no pressure and gradually relaxed. He loved bikes and would spend hours fixing them up working quietly alongside Jason or Joseph. We attended Children's Services meetings with both Harry and his mum and supported both of them. We were there for him whenever he needed help. When his bike was broken we would be there to pick him up, or we would turn up at home when he was too down even to get up in the morning. Constantly we helped him find the positives in his life. When quiet opportunities arose we would help him to the realisation that parents are human and mess up just like anyone else; you can love them but you don't have to be like them or make the same mistakes as them.

Life was always going to be difficult for Harry because that was his character. After leaving us, he did go to college and then he found work; he gave his mum less grief and found ways to spend time with dad.

17 Barry
handling rage

It felt like the pool ball had missed her head by millimetres but in reality it was well clear, probably at least a metre. "And that's how he aimed it," Liz told herself. She had no doubt that he could have cracked her skull open with it, if that had been what he intended. She glanced sideways at the dent it had made in the door she had just closed behind her. The ball was now rolling back across the workshop floor. Vannessa stooped forward from where she was guarding the door to the office, scooped up the pool ball and put it safely in her pocket. Barry, backside propped against the pool table in the centre of the room, juggling two pool balls, looked from one to the other of his gaolers, menacingly, as though making up his mind which he was going to attack next. His arm shot out in Vannessa's direction but the ball didn't leave his hand. Flint-faced, she didn't even blink let alone flinch. He spun, and hurled the ball harmlessly into an unoccupied corner of the room. This one rolled back towards Liz who, just as Vannessa had done, pocketed it.

"OK," thought Liz. "There were a few moments of real rage back then when he could have done anything, but that's passed. He's already got it under control but he doesn't know how to get himself out of this situation."

Another pool ball exploded off the far wall, bounced off a lathe and disappeared under the bike trailer. Liz looked across at Vannessa who met her glance and nodded. Long practiced familiarity told Liz that Vannessa would keep quiet. Hostage negotiation was Liz's job. Everyone was safe. Paul and Tony had efficiently cleared the workshop of the young people who had followed Barry in order to rubber neck at his rage and see what he might do next. The workshop was sealed. Barry wasn't going anywhere. She knew no one would have called the police. And what would they do in this situation? Pepper spray? Tasers? Yet there was nothing as powerful as words. She could handle this.

"Barry, it's ok," said Liz quietly. "I understand."

"Fuck off, Liz," he spat venomously, and then hurled another ball at the harmless corner.

"Barry, trust me," began Liz again even more quietly. "There's nothing we can't get sorted."

"Shut it, Liz, yer bitch," he screamed.

"Barry I don't know what kicked all this off but there's nothing we can't talk about. I need you to take a deep breath, keep calm and come into the office with me. We'll have a sit down, a cup of tea and you can tell me all about it." All this was delivered quietly, only just audibly, slowly and in her deepest, huskiest voice.

Barry changed tack. "Stop doing that," he yelled. "I'm not stupid. I know what you're doing. Stop doing that 'calm me down' voice!"

Liz suppressed the urge to laugh, and the urge to apologise. She remained quiet as he launched into a rant about how he hated her, hated Respect, hated all the other kids, hated his family, hated his 'shitty life'. Eventually he ran out of steam, swept the rest of the balls onto the floor, leant forward onto the table and sobbed into the baize. Liz approached, tentatively touched him on the shoulder and got no adverse reaction. She spoke softly and reassuringly to him. It was over.

Liz led Barry away from the unit and spent most of the day with him. They went down to the park. Having gone on the swings, they sat on a bench together, and they talked. They talked all day.

That evening the staff meeting was devoted to Barry. Liz provided Barry's version of events, Paul told the rest of the tale or as much of it as he had observed or gleaned from the other young people.

Before he came to us Paul had done an impressive variety of jobs that had given him a huge range of people skills. He'd worked for a bank, an insurance company, been a road worker and a nightclub doorman. He was doing a degree as a mature student when he turned up for a trial and possible part-time work.

He was a natural leader of young people and we took him on instantly. When he graduated we gave him a full-time job. He had life experience in bucket loads and a street awareness that meant no youngster ever got the better of him. He managed them with humour and when necessary was a master of the put-down - learnt through managing nightclub queues - that would have everyone rolling with laughter, staff and young people, apart from the victim and Liz who would give him a furious ticking off. Always his own greatest critic, Paul would take the point that these were children and needed to be treated as such. Strong, energetic, gentle and patient, Paul would do anything for anyone.

Paul had taken the lead with Barry since he arrived a few weeks earlier. It had been hard work. Barry had been feral for a long time. He'd lived on the streets, sofa surfing around the houses of mates, occasionally returning to his mum's or to his nan's. He hadn't been near a mainstream school for more than a year. He should have already triggered numerous trip wires as an extremely vulnerable child, but it was his involvement in 'county lines' that had drawn him to the attention of a raft of agencies. He was now in care and attending Respect regularly.

He made it clear when he joined us that he did not want to be there. He turned up every day because he had to, but made no effort to join in with activities. On some days he was left at the unit with Paul who, slowly but surely, began to find cracks in Barry's hard veneer. What swung it was a mutual interest in boxing. Paul talked about his own boxing career and when Barry, in turn, started talking about how he had got involved in boxing with his dad years before, Paul had the opening he needed. Before long he had Barry talking about his family and how his life had started to go all wrong. Paul then used his new relationship and the trust that had developed, to get Barry to try new activities, to mix with the other young people and to start thinking about how to create a future for himself. This was as far as we'd got before this day of anger.

That morning a new girl called Debbie had started. Debbie had been put in the same taxi as Barry and, according to her, he

111

had been absolutely charming. She had been nervous about coming to Respect4us, and was delighted to have company in the taxi, to have someone to tag along with who could show her the ropes. She said that when they walked in together he completely changed. He ignored her, and then, when she followed him into the kitchen, he was rude about her to the other boys. When she got upset he laughed at her. So she threw a piece of bread at him. The kitchen was full of youngsters all getting their own breakfasts, so when Barry responded by throwing a bowl of cereal at Debbie lots of other people got sprayed. Within seconds a full-scale food chucking war had broken out. Paul, Tony and Denise were on the scene and instantly calming things down. However, in the melee Barry had reached for a slice of bread on the floor and someone had trodden on his fingers. That's when he lost all control and began lashing out at all and sundry. Paul quickly had him corralled with only one escape route and that was out into the workshop. Barry took this route, Paul followed and then all the on-lookers. As Barry stood facing his tormentors, screaming at them in rage, Paul bundled the young people back through the door. It was at this point that Liz arrived, closed the door and stood there guarding it.

Now Liz took up the story, describing what had happened in the workshop and what she had learned from Barry through their conversations that day. It was time for decisions. Paul argued strongly that he was making progress with Barry and nothing should be done to de-rail that. Liz felt that she had made a lot of progress that day in winning Barry's trust and could see that this was a young person they could have a big impact on. All agreed that this was a hiccup and they needed to move on from it quickly. However, it had been extremely dangerous and there had to be some sort of consequence, albeit light touch. It was agreed that Barry would not be allowed back just for the following day and the usual letters sent. Things had actually got a lot more bureaucratic in recent weeks and there was now a lengthy form that had to be filled out in triplicate for the local authority. More paperwork, thought Liz, groaning to herself.

This day proved a turning point for Barry and the rest of his time with us was very positive. He began cooking and would delight in preparing Mediterranean style meals for everyone that always seemed to contain huge amounts of olive oil and garlic. He worked well with a small group of Year 11s who were focused on college applications. He did a lot of research work, finding out about work on the North Sea rigs and then began to send out his CV to companies that might be prepared to give him an apprenticeship. Contact was made with both his mum and grandmother and they began to come in for meetings. His nan helped him get all the information together for his CV and helped send them out. He was offered a place at college and left us with hope that he did have a future.

18 Debbie

making sense of It all

Following the anger day, Liz and Denise sat down to talk to Debbie. We felt Debbie had been rather neglected on her first day at Respect4us. So now the aim was partly to get to know her a little and partly to help her make sense of what had happened the previous day. From her point of view the day had started well through meeting a really nice boy in her taxi and had then deteriorated rapidly. She thought that she had in some way been the cause of what had happened, though how was still a complete mystery to her.

"Yesterday was your first day with us," said Liz, "and it was all more confusing and chaotic than we would have liked it to have been for you. We are really sorry about that, Debbie, and wanted to tell you it's not like that every day. Today is about us getting to know you."

"Is Barry here today?" Debbie asked.

"No, we've asked him to stay at home today."

"What....?.... What did I do wrong?"

"Nothing, absolutely nothing! It was not your fault."

"It's boys," interrupted Denise. "Boys are just a complete mystery. To me, anyway. I've lived with my husband and son for twenty-five years now and I still don't get them."

"Yes, it's nothing to do with you Debbie. It's a boy thing," added Liz. "I've got two sons, and I've worked with a lot of boys over the years so I think I know how they work. They're quite different to us girls."

Liz went on, "So what do I think happened yesterday? Barry has got a big heart and inside he's a really nice, kind boy. Whoever you were, he would have been friendly and helpful when you got in the taxi. But you're not just anyone, you're just starting at Respect and he goes there already, so he's going to want to tell you all about it. On top of that you're a really nice person and a very pretty girl. What boy his age is not going to respond to that and try to be nice?"

"Yes, but when we got here he was horrible. I don't understand," said Debbie miserably.

"Yes, well this is what you have to understand about boys and how they are so different to us. What their mates think, or what other boys think, is much more important to them than their relationship with a girl. Especially at that age. So however much Barry liked you, he didn't want to show that to the other boys. And - this is the real nub of the boy mystery - he thinks that if he is thought by the others to be soft on a girl, that will be seen as a weakness. They will tease him, make fun of him - and most boys dread that more than anything in the world. So when you follow him around like you're his girlfriend, or at least like you are good mates, then he feels he has to react against that - he has to put you down, or lose face in front of his mates. He wants to be seen by them as a hard man, a tough guy and not some soppy, love-struck kid. That's why he was so horrible to you."

Everyone thought about this for a moment.

"Do you get it?" asked Liz.

"Maybe," replied Debbie. "Are boys really that weird?"

"Afraid so," said Liz. "Just remember that Barry probably really likes you. It wasn't personal."

"So don't give up on him," added Denise.

"Now let's hear about you," said Liz. "How do you come to be with us? What do you want to get out of coming here?"

It wasn't just boys that were confusing to Debbie. She seemed confused about her own storyline which would change depending on her audience and which group she was trying to get in with. So what she told Liz and Denise that morning was different to the account of herself that Denise overheard her telling the other girls later in the day.

At lunchtime she announced that she was going out to KFC. Denise, who we had decided was to be her key worker, very firmly, but politely, said that was not going to happen and that we sat down to lunch together. If someone really couldn't eat in public - and we frequently had children with eating disorders - then we would arrange for them to eat on their own in an office.

115

We talked beforehand about what everyone liked to eat and as far as possible agreed on a menu for the week ahead. Everyone had the opportunity to join in the cooking from time to time. Breakfast was a free-for-all but lunch was always a sit down family meal in which everyone was expected to take part. Eventually, Denise got Debbie to sit down at the table with her and to eat lunch.

The next day, before lunch was called, Denise realised that Debbie had gone missing and straightaway worked out where she had gone. Levi - younger and fitter than everyone else - was dispatched to chase after her. Liz followed at a more sedate pace. Levi caught up with her at KFC where she had already bought her food. When they met up with Liz on their way back Debbie got a second ticking off. Debbie said she understood but to underline it Liz decided to telephone home.

Debbie lived with her dad. He answered the phone:
"Hello?"
"Hello. Is that Mr Smith? This is Liz from Respect4us, Debbie's alternative provision."
"Yeh?"
"Slight issue with Debbie this morning …. which I wanted to discuss with you."
"What's she done now?"
"Nothing too serious, don't worry. She went off premises at lunchtime to get a meal from KFC. It's just that we always cook together and eat together. Apart from anything else it's a question of her safety if we don't know where she is. She had been told that she was not to go and she understood that."
"How'd she pay for it?"
"She had money."
"Who from?"
"I don't know. I assumed you gave her money."
"No, definitely not! I bet she took it again out of my wallet. I'll have her hide when she gets home. I warned her last time."
"As far as we're concerned it's a minor issue. Just have a quiet word with her please. She's got it now and doesn't need punishing any more."

116

"Don't tell me what to do with my daughter! What kind of operation are you lot running anyway? It's bloody obvious you can't control those kids."

"We talk to our children, Mr Smith. We are teaching them to make sensible choices. There are always consequences when they misbehave or break the rules. But what we don't do is use any kind of physical force on them."

"You're a fucking waste of space and time. She should be in school not pissing about wasting her time with you jokers."

The line went dead.

Liz's next move was to report to the pupil referral unit that we would not be telephoning Debbie's home again for any reason but would report any concerns we had about her just to them. She followed this up as required with a written record of concern. Our concern was that we should not ever do anything to make Debbie's life at home any more difficult than it already was. In fact Debbie didn't do it again and there was never cause to make any further report about her behaviour. However this incident did have consequences.

A week or two later, at the end of one day, Paul was called out by a taxi driver who wanted help with Debbie because she was refusing to get in his taxi. It seems he had demanded she put her bag in the front seat and we suspect he had done this rather rudely. She had refused. Paul decided to ignore the fact that this was not the first time she'd been asked to do it and that she knew perfectly well why it was. He explained again that the taxis had this rule because some young people in the past had got lighters or illicit items out of their bags while in transit. He said he knew she would never cause a problem like this but it was one of those rules that everyone had to obey. With huge diplomatic skill, he said to the driver that Debbie was worried that he might take something out of her bag so could he, the driver, please reassure Debbie that this wouldn't happen. The driver did this grumpily and Debbie then put her bag on the front seat and climbed in the back. Paul had noticed that throughout this exchange Debbie had been silently weeping, so as he closed the front cab door he said to the driver, "Please be kind."

So what had upset Debbie? - apart from a taxi driver who thought he could speak to young people in a tone that he would never use with adults? Paul found out what had happened at the staff debriefing meeting, and was able to add his observations of the taxi incident.

Our office had received a call from the pupil referral unit in the early afternoon to say that a social worker was coming in to interview Debbie. The only problem with this was that the social worker had already arrived and we had had no time at all to prepare Debbie who didn't know what it was about. She was understandably worried, shocked and upset. Denise had had great difficulty in persuading her to come through to the office to meet the social worker. When she finally came in it was to be grilled insensitively by the social worker about how she lived with her dad. Did he have a cooker? How did they eat their meals? Did he have a washing machine? Were her clothes clean?

It all got too much for Debbie and she stormed out of the office. Interestingly, it was Barry who stopped her leaving the premises and persuaded her to come back.

At this point Liz, who had been busy all afternoon with other matters, joined the meeting. She immediately became Debbie's champion, pointing out that as one of our cleanest and most tidily presented young people, Debbie was justifiably offended by the implication that she was dirty. She said that if Children's Services wanted to provide the family with a new cooker and new washing machine she was sure that would be welcomed. At this point the taxis had started to arrive and Liz gave Debbie permission to leave.

The social worker was not happy:

"I've not finished and now I'll have to come back."

"Of course," said Liz. "That's absolutely fine. But if you want to talk to Debbie, next time you prearrange your visit, giving us several days' notice. I understand you have concerns about the family and her home, but this is becoming a safe space for Debbie where she feels settled and secure, and I am not having that disrupted so you can fill in your forms and write your reports. She is a vulnerable child and needs to be treated as such. You will come in future at a time that suits us and when we can provide Debbie with the support she will clearly need."

"Well said, Liz," declared Paul in the staff meeting. "And that explains why Debbie was so upset having to deal with a rude taxi driver."

Liz had been too busy to be present at the start of the meeting with the social worker because she had been dealing with another girl. Sarah had been due to start that morning but mum had been unable to get her out of the house until the early afternoon, and had then driven her to Respect. Now Sarah was refusing to get out of the car. Paul came out to help. Mum and one of her friends occupied the front seats and Sarah was in the back of the car. All of them remained seated. Paul, who is a very big man, had to squat down low to talk to them all. Mum and friend became quite flirtatious while Sarah sat sullenly in the back looking in the opposite direction. Increasingly irritated at being unable to get past the two women to talk directly to Sarah, and slightly embarrassed by the silliness of these two, Paul retreated to get Liz as reinforcement.

It turned out that mum was the younger sister of two girls Liz and I had worked with years before when in mainstream school. So Liz had a lovely long chat with mum, while squatting on the ground beside the car. Sarah, now crying, remained in the back of the car. Eventually, Liz got past mum and was able to talk to Sarah directly.
"So talk to me Sarah. Why don't you want to join us? I'm sure your mum is wonderful company but don't you want to spend some time with young people your own age?"
"It's all boys here. You got no girls."
These were the first words Sarah had uttered. Progress, thought Liz.
"Well," Liz said, aloud, "you don't look to me like the sort of girl who needs all female company. We do have some rather nice boys here and actually we do have a number of girls. We've

got a girl called Debbie here this afternoon and she's only just started."

"But it's rubbish. I told them I wanted to go to college," she said, petulantly.

"OK but the referral unit felt you weren't ready for that. You weren't coping with school so they thought you would struggle in college. Now, I don't know anything about you, only what they have told me. Trust me, if I work with you for a few days and I think you're ready for college I will tell them so. They've said to me, you need some help learning how to manage your emotions and behaviour so that, when you do go to college, we can all be certain that you're going to be successful."

Sarah said nothing, so Liz changed tack:

"You look just like your aunt Laura. She was a real looker and had a beautiful deep voice."

"Ugh! I hate her posh voice. She's always so snobby."

"Well, she was unusual among my girls because she was so well spoken. You'd never hear Laura swear. Her mum, your nan, used to terrify me."

Sarah's mum laughed, "I know what you mean, me too."

Liz kept the chat going for an hour and a half until she felt her knees had completely seized up. She eased herself upright. Mum took this as a hint to put her foot down for once.

"Come on," she said, "Sarah just get out the bloody car and give it a go."

"Don't you start!" said Sarah forcefully. "What do you know about anything? You're fucking useless!"

"Don't you give me your lip, girl!" shouted mum back over her shoulder.

"OK, that's enough everyone," said Liz. "What I suggest is that you go home now Sarah and come back tomorrow. In the morning I'll come out to meet you and then you'll come into the unit with me and we'll have no nonsense. Do we have a deal?"

"OK," said Sarah.

Liz stuck her hand through the window and they shook on it.

The car drove off. Liz returned to the office and was immediately sucked into the meeting with the social worker.

The next day everyone rallied around to support Debbie and to reassure her that the previous day's unpleasant encounter with the social worker would not be repeated. Barry had been enrolled as a supporter and, rising to the responsibility, he was particularly attentive. Debbie in turn was enrolled to support Sarah who appeared mid-morning and did get out of the car this time. She spent the rest of the day with Debbie and Barry.

The following year the three of them all started college together.

19 Zara

fetal alcohol syndrome

As the reputation of Respect for dealing with the most intractable behaviour cases grew, more and more difficult cases began to come our way. We didn't always take them. We had learned, when dealing with Susan, that it was dangerous to take on a case unless we were confident we had the resources to cope. Normally this would mean that we had two members of staff who could work full-time with the child. We would never risk putting one of these extremely difficult children in with a group unless we were sure it was going to work.

Children's Services had asked the pupil referral unit for advice about Zara. The referral unit had recommended us for the job. They qualified their response both to the client and to us by saying we were unlikely to be successful but if anyone could make any progress with her it would be us.

We were flattered and we loved a challenge, but we had to think very hard about it. The commission had come at a difficult time when we had been unusually busy. Staff were fully stretched across all our units. Liz knew, because of the difficulty of the task, and because no one else could be spared, that she would have to take on the job herself. Clearly there would need to be two people to do the work and Mark was her choice as her co-worker

Mark had been the premises caretaker at the school where Liz and I had previously worked. It was Liz who recognised how good he was at working with young people and had been on to him for some time to give up his secure employment in school and to come and work with us. His understanding of children came from years of experience as a foster parent. He was calm, patient, unshockable and had the mature judgement to size up people and situations. He could anticipate behaviours so that nothing children ever did caught him by surprise. When Liz

122

decided to take on this latest challenging assignment, it was the unflappable Mark she wanted.

Zara's story starts after we had been working with her for nearly a month and it had proved just as difficult as everyone had predicted.

Mark was squatting on the bank watching the two of them in the stream, Liz and the girl. Liz was crouching forward, poised, watching the minnows dart about in a pool, ready to scoop one out with the net on the cane she held. The girl stood behind and to the side of her, watching, fascinated. Liz's arm shot forward. The net scooped into the pool. Up it came, streaming water. No fish.

Liz stood tall, stretching her back, and looked at the girl.
"Want to have a try, Zara?" she asked.
The girl slowly reached out and took the net. Liz remained at her side as the two of them resumed their watch of the little fish.

Mark had remained on the bank observing, as their previous visit to the stream had ended with him being pushed from behind by Zara and going headlong into the water. He had agreed with Liz that this time he would sit out and yell a warning to her if Zara looked like repeating the trick. Her behaviour was just so unpredictable. She appeared placid at this moment, as though butter wouldn't melt in her mouth, he thought. She certainly didn't look as though she could do much damage to anyone. She was small, and with a head that seemed small even in relation to her slight body. Her small eyes often had a vacant look about them. Fetal alcohol syndrome was not a condition he had come across in all his years of fostering children. In this area of work, he mused, you just keep on learning new things. At any rate now at long last they had perhaps found something that she liked doing.

Zara had a severe form of fetal alcohol syndrome. Her alcoholic and drug addicted birth mother, in one of her short spells outside prison, had managed to get herself pregnant. We

123

knew none of the details of this, just enough to have some understanding of the child's disabilities. Typically a child with FAS will have damage to the brain, spinal column and sometimes their major organs. This will almost certainly mean they have learning difficulties. We didn't know a lot about Zara's physical and learning disabilities but it was our brief to get her to engage with the world in some small way, to become a little more socially adaptable, to communicate a little more, to discover new activities that she could enjoy doing. Our aims were very limited but frequently we felt we had bitten off more than we could chew.

Zara lived in a semi-secure children's home that had been designed for two residents. She was currently the only resident as she had driven the other one away. She had not been out of the home for months. The hope was that if we could build a relationship, and manage to winkle her out of the house, we could show her how to interact with the world outside sufficiently to enable her eventually to be able to benefit from attending a special school.

When Liz and Mark turned up at the home for their first session they were admitted by the children's home manager. As they stood introducing themselves in the hallway Zara came out of the kitchen.
"Zara, these are the people I was telling you about," said the manager.
"Hello Zara, I'm Liz."
"Fuck off! I don't know you," said Zara, heading for the staircase.
"They are going to take you out," said the manager.
"No!......I'm not going out with ...them," said Zara as she turned and then ran up the stairs.

Liz decided not to invade her space any further than she had done already. She sat on the bottom stairs, every so often calling out to Zara trying to engage her. Mark went into the kitchen to chat with the staff and to try to get more information about them and their charge. The kitchen floor was littered with food and broken crockery.

One of the staff noticed Mark looking at the mess:

" Zara took exception to something I said." He smiled, "Not for the first time."

The second day was an almost exact repeat of the first day. In the kitchen Mark learned that there was to be no coffee that morning as the previous evening Zara had smashed every cup in the house.

On the third day they went straight into the kitchen to drink coffee and talk to the staff without making any effort to talk to Zara. This time it wasn't food splattered all over the floor and cupboards, it was paint. But there were cups!

"We tried an art class," said the manager.

On the fourth day they met her as they came in.

"Fuck off!" and she disappeared up the stairs.

They went through for their usual meeting in the kitchen.

Coming out a little later they found a mattress had slid down the stairs. The manager said Zara had taken to doing this to get attention.

As Liz stood at the foot of the stairs, gazing up, she felt a hand around her ankle.

"Oooh," she shrieked. Then she laughed. "You made me jump!"

She was rewarded by a little titter of laughter in return from under the mattress.

Liz settled down on the floor and began to talk about whatever came into her head. She talked about Respect and what we did and what all the other young people were like and some of the silly things they did. Eventually she realised that a head had appeared from under the mattress.

"Would you like to see pictures of some of our young people?" Liz asked.

The head nodded.

"Here," said Liz, getting her phone out, "have a look at our facebook page."

Zara took the phone and began scrolling through pictures as Liz talked about them.

During this episode Mark had come out of the kitchen, placed a coffee cup beside her and then scuttled away quickly. A while later all the staff came out without a sound and stepping politely over Liz's legs, went their way. Noticing Mark standing there, Liz introduced him then, getting up quickly, announced it was time to go and they left.

"Made some progress there," she said as Mark shut the front door behind them. "Don't want to push our luck. Let's see what happens next time."

On the fifth visit they were greeted by the usual words but perhaps said not quite as aggressively:

"Fuck off out of my home."

"Quite right," said Liz, "We are intruding in your home. We will wait in the car outside where you can see us."

After twenty minutes the manager came out. He said that Zara wanted them to come in. However he felt it was wrong that she was calling all the shots.

"Trust us," said Liz, "none of this can be forced."

He agreed to give them the benefit of the doubt and apologised for being grumpy.

"Zara had us up all night," he said. "Then in the early hours she smashed the fuse box and we had no electricity until an hour ago."

Liz and Mark met Zara in the sitting room with the manager. She didn't sit down but stood by the door. Eventually she agreed to come out with them as long as a member of the care staff came too. They agreed that they would return her to the home whenever she felt she needed to be back.

The sixth visit was the day they were finally to get her out of the house. However they didn't know this when they arrived. They were determined not to be greeted by a "fuck off" so they respected her space and remained in the car, tooting the horn to

126

get attention. They were rewarded by seeing a little face peeking out from behind a curtain. Liz then knocked on the door to make sure the staff were aware they were there and then returned to the car. Eventually a member of staff emerged followed cautiously and nervously by Zara.

It was a fine day and they had already decided they would go not very far to a stream in a meadow they knew about. The activity was to introduce her to 'tiddling', catching tiny fish in a net, something they knew always went down well with their younger ones.

By the end of the session she had not joined in at all so they were a little surprised that she wanted to repeat the activity when asked what she wanted to do next time. Liz began to understand that repetition was the key to managing Zara, and that any change to routine needed to be introduced almost imperceptibly to avoid throwing her into a panic.

So we return to Mark sitting on the stream bank, watching Liz still straightening her back, and Zara tentatively dipping the net in the pool. He was aware of a very strange droning, whirring noise getting louder and louder. Then he saw a black cloud coming out of the trees on the opposite bank. He called in alarm to Liz as he realised it was a swarm of bees. It took Liz a moment or two to see the danger and then she barked at Zara to freeze and not move a muscle. For a second or two, that seemed much longer, they were in the centre of the swarm, and then it had gone. Liz realised that Zara had done as she'd demanded. Some instinct for self-preservation had made her not argue, not fight, but do exactly the right thing. She seemed very excited by it and insisted they leave straight away to go home and tell the care staff about it.

So began a series of visits, on each of which they ended up back at the stream. They found that as long as they did exactly the same thing each time she would remain calm. Generally these outings were successful and all the time Mark and Liz were becoming more familiar, more acceptable, more trusted. There was one day dubbed by Mark as "poogate" when they arrived in the morning to find Zara had been in her room since the previous afternoon and was not coming out. She had been storing her faeces and when anyone went into her room she flung it at them! They didn't go out that day.

Finally, after many weeks of talking about the other young people and what they got up to, they persuaded Zara to come and see for herself. They chose a day when the unit was empty, all other staff and young people were out. They let Zara explore and become familiar with the layout of rooms. It was just the three of them and they kept the visit brief. They repeated this several times, and then introduced another member of staff and a few young people, hand-picked for their gentleness and calmness. Gradually the numbers were increased until Zara was experiencing a normal day at Respect. It didn't all go smoothly; there was the day she ripped down all the displays of work; the day she ran off up the road with staff in pursuit. But on the whole we felt we were making progress in getting her used to being in different situations and with different people.

Gradually we began to introduce the idea of going to school. Liz was burdened with many phone calls, meetings and planning sessions to make this happen. All pulled together - care home staff, the head and staff of the special school - as we went through the now familiar process of introducing Zara to a new experience. By the end of the year she was attending three days at the special school and two days at Respect4us. In September she was full-time at the special school and making phenomenal progress.

Towards the end of her time with us, we learned that there were adoptive parents who were pressing to have Zara back with them. She had not been at the special school for very long when the parents got their way. She moved back with them and within weeks all our careful work had fallen apart. Zara was back into care and her next move was out of the county. A year or so later she contacted us via Facebook to tell us that she was doing ok and liked living in Wales!

20 Younger children

the primary challenge

I had worked all my career in secondary education and in my ignorance I had once thought that misbehaving to the point where they got excluded from school was something that happened to children only when they became teenagers. In 2017-18 in England 1210 children were permanently excluded from primary school and the number had doubled in the previous five years. In the same year there were 66,000 fixed term exclusions. 156 of the permanent exclusions and 9300 of the fixed term exclusions were of children aged only 6. In Norfolk in 2017-18, 47 primary aged children were permanently excluded.[4]

As our success in turning children around grew, we began to come under pressure to work with younger children. We agreed because we were professionally intrigued to see if we could make a difference in this area that was completely new to us. There was a logic to it in that any intervention at age 15-16 is going to be too little too late; the earlier any intervention comes the more likely it is to have long-term impact.

To work with younger children we would need separate premises. We were already running two satellite units in towns 25 miles from the city and this was causing us logistical and management problems. We were beginning to lose something of our cohesion founded on the end of day meeting and shared ethos that was so intrinsic to our working practice. The staff, who worked at the very least in pairs in the satellites, were unable to get to our meetings. If we were to establish a primary base, it was essential that it was not too far away so we could meet regularly, and we could provide additional support whenever it was needed. In the end we hired a cabin in the beautiful parkland grounds of a nearby outdoor activity centre. It was extremely peaceful in

---

[4] UK Government statistics
https://www.gov.uk/government/collections/statistics-exclusions

surroundings that were full of wildlife and interest to younger children.

Liz established the new unit which was then run by Rachael who had been running one of our satellites. When she moved on, we asked Denise to take over. She was by then one of our longest standing members of staff and she had proved herself on many occasions. She was amazing in working one-to-one with the most needy young people and in winning their trust and confidence. She had an ability to see past outward behaviour and identify the real issues that were bothering a child. One of our best reflective practitioners, she would always listen to guidance, think about it and then invariably act on it. We felt she deserved her chance to run something of her own.

We selected Levi to help Denise run this little unit. I could write a chapter about Levi as one of Respect's greatest success stories. He came to us as a fourteen year old in our first year of operation. Unusually he had not been excluded from school. His school knew he had some great qualities but recognised his inability to sit still in a classroom, or to keep his mouth shut when talking was inappropriate. He was fearless, irrepressible and brimful of restless energy. They thought that if he was able to work off some of that energy with us, he might find it easier to settle to academic study on his other days in school.

Levi thrived as a student at Respect. He had a sense of humour and fun, and a sunny disposition that just couldn't be crushed. He caused us a number of headaches over his two years with us, but we all fed off his energy and enthusiasm and we recognised that he had an aptitude for leadership. From us he went on to college for three years, in his final year studying sport and fitness. Having some spare time in his week, he asked if he could return to help out as a volunteer. We saw immediately that he had a huge amount to offer and at the end of the year we offered him a job. In the five years since we first met him, Levi had matured. He had learned how to listen and keep his own counsel, how to be still and silent, how to observe and reflect. And yet he was still full of energy; he could run faster, play football longer, cycle further than any of our youngsters. He had the same energy and enthusiasm but had learnt how to use it to get others fired up; he had learnt leadership. When we started the primary unit his energy was the perfect foil for Denise's quiet support.

There were usually five children aged between 6 and 10 working at the primary unit. Using a seven-seater car the staff would drive around picking them all up in the morning. The addresses covered a large geographic area and so quite a lot of the day was spent in the car and this needed to be used as learning time. One member of staff would go to the door and when the child came out, send him or her to the car. It was then possible to speak to the parent or carer with the child out of earshot. This was an opportunity for either side to share information or to discuss jointly how they were handling different types of behaviour. We always saw our job as partly training the adults who were with the child for much longer than we were; of course we didn't always get things right and sometimes we just needed to listen to the parent or carer and learn from them. Meanwhile the child would have gone to the car and be chatting with the other member of staff and with the other children. It was even more the case with primary aged children that what we focused on was communication - talking about themselves, listening to others and sharing views, ideas, thoughts, activities and experiences. A lot of this went on in the car.

At the unit we followed much the same programme as the older children. First there would be food and drinks. Then we would talk about what had happened since they were last together. This might be about school or about home and we made it clear that we wanted to hear about the disasters and the triumphs and the boringly banal. At some point we would switch to discussing the activities for the day. These were energetic, physical and practical. There might be a run or brisk walk through the woods, supervised tree climbing, den making, or pond dipping. Later in the morning they might be building bird boxes or insect hotels.

Everyone had to keep a diary in which they were expected to write at least two or three sentences as well as doing drawings about what they had done that day. If the child was with us for long enough they would do a six week John Muir Award course.[5] This had been introduced originally by Rachael and worked really well with primary aged children. There was a logbook with activities all based around the environment and nature and its successful completion resulted in the award of a certificate that could be taken home. All this quieter study and book work went on before and after lunch.

The day always ended with more vigorous exercise - running around, playing football, cricket, frisbee throwing or haring through the maze. The journey home could be quiet or could involve social chat or sometimes the continuation of a debate that had gone on earlier.

Well that's how the day would have gone if these were ordinary, polite, well-behaved children. Of course they weren't, so the reality was not always like that. Sometimes a child would come in with a dark cloud over them and refuse to join in. One member of staff could then be engaged all day in trying to get the child to talk about what the problem was. Quite frequently two or more children could come in bringing upsets from home with them. On days like that it felt like there were not enough staff to go round. If the children who had started the day without issues were neglected for any length of time they would pretty soon have issues of their own. What all these children had in common was that they were very needy and very demanding. We began to see why they were so difficult to manage in schools where they were in large classes. Our staff were regularly hit, kicked and spat at - things that were generally taboo among the young people in our older units. On one occasion a child ran off and the staff had no option but to call for more help. After a case conference it was decided that this child was just too much of a risk and he didn't attend again.

---

[5] https://www.johnmuirtrust.org

Nicky was fairly typical of the children who came to us. He was aged 8, living in care with fairly elderly foster parents who were probably a bit out of their depth with him. We knew nothing about his birth parents but it was clear that he had had a very unsettled and troubled upbringing to date. He was difficult because we could never predict how he was going to behave. Some days he would be absolutely fine, would mix well with the others and join in with all the activities. On other days he would come in apparently unable to speak, and be completely withdrawn. Then at some point he could go berserk. He never hurt any of the other children or put them at risk in any way. Denise would stay with him but give him space so he couldn't do too much damage to himself or to property, if possible getting him outside into the open. Eventually he would calm down. This is where we became aware of the difference between 8 year olds and fifteen year olds. With our older ones we could usually start talking at some point after they had cooled down, to take them through what had happened, to explore the emotions and the feelings and the thoughts that had led to them running amok. Perhaps, it is possible to do this with an 8 year old but we just didn't have the skills to do it. For Denise hugs and physical reassurance would bring the child back to a state of calm and they could move on. It worked for her because she was 'mum'.

We never got to the bottom of Nicky's troubles and the loss of control occurred regularly. A particularly bad incident occurred shortly after they had picked him up one morning. Denise was driving - and she was normally the expert in calming Nicky down. Levi had been replaced that day by Sarah who was sitting in the middle of the second row of the car with Nicky on one side and another child on the other. With the car in motion Nicky removed his seat belt and began screaming. He swore, he spat and he punched Sarah when she tried to restrain him. Sarah kept very calm throughout. She didn't let him out of the car or his seat despite the flurry of punches and kicks. Denise stopped the car and phoned the carer. Nicky was calming down as they drove back to his home, where he remained that day. The next day he came in, he was absolutely fine.

133

Primary was a bit of an experiment for us. We never had the staffing to really get to the bottom of some of the issues we were faced with and it's hard to measure what success we had. I think we helped children learn social behaviour in an environment where they could relax a lot more than they could in school. There were very few rules to be obeyed and sitting still was required for only very short periods of time. When schools receive children there are very many behaviours that are expected and taken for granted. Of course we have all heard those apocryphal tales about children arriving in primary school without potty training. I don't know if these are true but it can't be surprising that children who have been abused or are from chaotic backgrounds or have had little consistency in their rearing arrive in school without manners, with little self control, with little or no understanding of social norms. To some children these things have to be taught before they can be expected to get to grips with the national curriculum.

Our work with these younger children came to an end because we could no longer afford to do it. We had neither the money nor the staff to continue as in the final years of Respect4us we pulled back to concentrate on our core activity in the city. A measure of our success might be that we never saw any of our primary children graduate to our units for secondary pupils.

21 Tony and Gary
county lines

Over the years in which we operated, we worked continually to educate young people about drugs. Educate is probably the wrong word because they often knew far more about drugs and the drug scene than we did and we all learned more from them than they did from us. We had in theory a zero tolerance approach. However, we usually took the line that it was far better to keep the young person with us, even knowing they were continually going to re-offend. What we tried to do was get across the damage they could do to themselves from getting involved in drug culture. We avoided the debate about whether or not weed was harmful in itself. Weed is now too ubiquitous in society and dope smoking is taken for granted as a normal part of life by young people and very often by their families. However we stressed that it was illegal and that it would never happen on our premises or in our time. We stressed the harm to their health, the long-term damage they could do to their future by getting a criminal record, the dangers of getting tempted to start taking harder drugs, and the potentially life-threatening consequences of getting drawn into gangs.

In the early days we were talking mainly about recreational dope smoking; in recent years things had got a lot more serious with the advent of so-called 'county lines'. Key to the operation of these national drug distribution networks are vulnerable young people. It was inevitable that the children we worked with would be vulnerable to recruitment by county lines gangs. They were not in school, their futures were already bleak, they were bored and already living on the margins of society. As regular users of weed they were already possibly in debt or 'bondage' to local dealers. Young people, excluded from school and with too much time on their hands, will inevitably be drawn together with similar young people. That's the origin of a teenage gang, and reasonably harmless to begin with. They all smoke weed and source it jointly. They come to the attention of dealers who offer them a plentiful supply in return for running errands. It doesn't take long and they are in deep, becoming foot soldiers protecting a patch or a postcode from rival gangs. They arm themselves with knives. And soon most of the kids in a neighbourhood are carrying knives for protection.

At Respect we came across the impact of county lines on a regular basis. Tony was thirteen and had been coming to us for a few months. He seemed to be getting on well and there had been talk about getting him back into mainstream school. Then he suddenly stopped attending. We followed up rapidly, as we always did, with a home visit. His mum told us he had fallen out with his friends. He told us we were too far away and he couldn't walk in. At the time he was one of our closest students, probably no more than five to ten minutes walk away. Nonetheless we offered to put him on our minibus collection round. This did the trick and he started attending again. We knew there was something more to it and set to work to get to the bottom of what was troubling him.

It didn't take Liz long to get him talking. His love of weed had got him excluded from school. Far from learning a lesson from this, lack of routine and structure in his life had led him to increase his consumption. He'd got involved with a local gang (a group his own age who his mum saw as his 'friends') as a means of supplying his habit. This gang would run errands, collecting packages and making deliveries to addresses in their local area. With his place at Respect some structure and hope began to come back into Tony's life and when there was a realistic prospect of returning to school he decided to get out of the gang.

The gang didn't like this rejection. They hung around outside his house until he came out. They knocked him to the ground and collectively kicked him. Since then he'd been too scared to set foot outside his door. There was no one in this gang older than fourteen!

Gary was another very young teenager who had been involved in gangs. He was thirteen when he came to us, and was black with a striking Afro hairstyle. He had been brought up in London in a single parent family. He loved his mum and missed her a great deal when he was sent to Norfolk - this we knew from spending a lot of time helping him write and send her letters and cards. In London mum had been busy working and looking after younger children, and Gary had suffered from neglect. Like so many other children he had found the support and companionship he needed on the streets. By the age of twelve he was in a gang and got himself arrested after chasing a man down a street with a knife in his hand. Mum was pregnant and was told by her social worker that either Gary or the baby would be taken into care. In the end it was decided that Gary would go to live with an aunt in Great Yarmouth and that's how we came to be involved with him.

Gary was angry, sad and very confused. He seemed as a child to have had little or no guidance from loving adults. So far in his life he had tried to survive on his own as best he could. The life he had in London had seemed to make sense to him at the time; but now it had all fallen apart and he struggled to understand what had happened. It was as though he was only just beginning to wake up to the fact that the way he had lived was not normal; that it was not how all other children lived. He loved his mum and it had never entered his mind that he was the victim of neglect.

This was serious trauma and Liz did her best to help him through it. She spent hours with Gary just listening. He talked about his life in London on the streets. He described how he and friends at his primary school had begun running for a local gang, and how the leaders of the gang had become the significant adults in their lives. He looked up to them because they seemed successful, confident and caring. They were the people he went to for advice or help when he had a problem. His mum, by contrast, was always worried, harassed, short-tempered and made him feel he was just a nuisance. Now he missed her desperately, and he missed his mates. He was lonely.
"Can't you get another black kid here, Liz? I hate being the only one."

That gave Liz a lot to think about.

Our satellite unit in Yarmouth was in its dying days and we had begun bussing the remaining young people up to Norwich. Liz knew we couldn't afford to keep it open for long but as a temporary measure she moved Gary back to Yarmouth so that he could get a lot of adult attention. He was there with just one other thirteen year old boy with whom he developed a friendship. The boys decided they wanted to learn to cook and they experimented with all sorts of cuisine. Gradually Gary lost all his gangster talk and began to seem happier in himself. After a few weeks he was offered a place in a mainstream school and began there full-time. Before he left he told Liz that his 'boys' in London had wished him well when he had to leave, and they'd said that he was being given a real chance in life by being sent to Yarmouth.

"I didn't agree with them at the time,' he said, "but now I think maybe they were right. I'm going to make a fresh start at this school."

Result! thought Liz.

'County Lines' had become widely talked about by all the concerned agencies and we got new instructions from Children's Services and the schools we worked with. Every incident involving drugs that we came across now had to be reported to the police from whom we had to get a report number that was then logged with the school. We warned our young people that this would happen and the next time a youngster was found rolling up behind the unit, the dope was confiscated and the report made.

"What should we do with the confiscated dope?" we asked.

"Hand it in to the police," came back the answer from the school.

In the old days we would have just waited till Friday and the friendly visit of our PCSOs but now we had to find a police station. That's actually quite hard to do these days without travelling a long way. We were eventually referred to a station on another industrial estate. That's where Liz went with her bag of weed. She takes up the story:

It was an anonymous looking building not dissimilar to our own industrial unit. I stood at what seemed to be the front door and politely rang the bell. There was no reply and it was now raining. After a long wait a guy came out and nodded me in, even holding the door open for me but otherwise saying nothing and he disappeared. I was thinking that handing something in to the police is really not easy.

I looked around and noticed another bell which I rang.

A very serious looking and sounding man then appeared.

"How did you get in here?" he demanded officiously.

"Through the door?" I said timidly.

This was not the right answer apparently and the fierce man disappeared.

A police constable then came out and told me more gently that I had no right to be inside the building. I explained that I really didn't want to be there but I had been instructed by a school that I worked with that I had to hand in dope removed from a child. I was doing as I had been told. He rolled his eyes and said they had no interest in receiving dope and suggested I destroy it myself or tell the school to do so. I was then shown out.

How do you destroy dope? Flushing it down the loo doesn't seem like a very responsible thing to do but in the absence of an incinerator that's what I tried. Not a clever idea! It won't flush. We all felt very uncomfortable having dope sitting around on our premises, even locked in a secure cabinet.

It was a little frustrating to find ourselves in the front line working with the most obvious victims of 'county lines' but with so little practical support. There was great concern about the issue both at the national and local levels. Resources were being shifted around and money spent to address the problem but none of it seemed to be coming our way. We carried on doing what we always did - talking to children and doing everything we could to keep them safe and to steer them away from trouble. From time to time we were invited to meetings where the grown-ups would pontificate and all feel as though they were doing something but none of it impacted on what the young people were doing. We were asked to report our concerns and from time to time we did so but nothing ever seemed to come of it. All our children were victims or potential victims and we were concerned about all of them.

As we saw it the issue was all about social exclusion. And for our young people social exclusion perhaps didn't begin with school exclusion but was certainly confirmed by it. School exclusions kept on increasing and as 'austerity' bit harder the money available for alternative provision got less and less. Where were all these displaced and hopeless young people going to end up if not on the streets involved in gangs, drugs and knife crime?

Conclusions

We closed our doors at the end of 2019. The main reason for this was our precarious financial situation. Money had been a problem from the start in 2010. We were not funded by any government agency. I've mentioned already how we received grants from BBC Children In Need and from the National Lottery but these could only be used for special projects and could never fund our basic running costs - wages, rent, vehicles, insurance and utilities. All our income came from the schools who asked us to help provide an alternative curriculum for the children whose needs they couldn't meet themselves.

The first ten years of this century was a golden decade for educational funding in my experience, and in the first years of Respect4us, from 2010, schools still had a reasonable level of funding and could afford to send children to us. We minimised our costs by exploiting the commitment and dedication of our staff who all took home little more than the minimum wage. In return everyone had a say in the running of the business and all received equal reward.

As demand for our services increased, we set up satellite units to reduce the distance some of our young people had to travel. In our second year we had a 'pop-up" satellite in Swaffham, serving the west of the county, operating for three days a week, first out of a community hall and then out of the rugby ground clubhouse. The following year we opened a permanent unit in Great Yarmouth to serve the east of the county. When we opened our unit for primary aged children, Respect had reached a peak in its growth, working with forty to fifty children each day. It was at that point that the "austerity" cuts in government spending really began to bite and schools found it increasingly difficult to find any money to send us their children. Inevitably, exclusions increased. In 2012/13 Norfolk's permanent exclusion rate had fallen to a low of 19 pupils in every 10,000. By 2015/16 this rate had more than doubled to 41 per 10,000, one of the highest rates in the country, and by the final year of the decade it was still at 35 per 10,000 (UK Government education statistics[6]).

As our financial difficulties increased we closed our satellite operations, reduced our staff, and retrenched in Norwich. It was still not sustainable. We began 2019-20 with a skeleton staff and when the numbers did not pick up as they usually did during the autumn term, we decided to close our last unit and shut down.

The remaining staff who wanted to carry on working with young people had no difficulty in selling their skills to other alternative providers. It wasn't the same as Respect but they had better pay and more certainty of being paid. The pupil referral unit found other placements for the few young people who remained with us.

It was Barry (ch17) who asked, very reasonably, "So why are you closing Respect?"
"Well it's not easy running a business, you know," Liz replied. "Also my husband has retired, and at my age I would really like to be doing something less stressful."
"Fair enough," he said and laughed.
"But I will always champion your age group, you know," she said.
"Yeh," he said. "We need it 'cos people always look down on us..... OK, I dress like this - joggers, hoody, trainers - and we hang around in groups, and maybe we look scary, but you know that we're not all bad." He added, laughing, "Yeh, you go and tell 'em that, Liz."
"You know, I think Dom and I are going to write a book about it," said Liz.

---

[6] https://explore-education-statistics.service.gov.uk/

what we achieved

Over ten years we had created from scratch an organisation that had touched the lives of several thousand young people. Most of them came to us at very low points in their lives and we demonstrated to them that we cared about them. We gave most of them confidence and self belief and showed them ways they could improve their lives and create futures for themselves. We supported children suffering from abuse and neglect. We turned some away from drugs and crime. We made most of them physically and mentally stronger. We taught social skills, communication skills, cooking and healthy eating. We introduced them to many new sports and recreational activities. We helped them discover what they were good at and pointed the way to developing their talents. Many went on from us into college and apprenticeships. Some went back into school where they were better equipped to settle down, behave themselves and make use of the opportunities afforded by school. Some have gone on to start businesses to support themselves and others. A lot have become parents themselves and, due to the work we did with them, the next generation stand a much better chance of being successful.

We remain very proud of this work. It was immensely difficult. These are often very hard kids to like or to love. Some would seem to many of our fellow citizens to have no redeeming features at all.

Respect4us made a difference. We proved again and again that there is no child who can't be rescued, who can't be turned around, and helped to become someone who contributes positively to society. On the rare occasion we failed it was due to lack of resources and in particular access to the right skilled specialists and treatment programmes.

The death of Victoria Climbie in 2000, and the inquiry by Lord Laming that followed, shocked and shamed the nation. It led to the development of the 'Every Child Matters' policy' which laid down five rights for all our children:

to be healthy, to stay safe, to enjoy and achieve, to make a positive contribution, and to achieve economic well-being.

The 'Every Child Matters' Green Paper published in September 2003 still makes powerful reading seventeen years on. Building on Lord Laming's recommendations, it asserted that:

"Child protection cannot be separated from policies to improve children's lives as a whole."[7]

From 2010 the Coalition Government changed the emphasis from 'Every Child Matters' to one of 'Safeguarding' which is now supposed to be at the forefront of the mind of anyone who works with children. In its implementation the aim of 'Safeguarding' has become narrowed to merely seeking signs of physical or sexual abuse. I prefer the wider embrace of 'Every Child Matters' and its five rights. The children who crossed the threshold of Respect4us had no expectation of ever benefitting from those rights. I know we had only to raise the alarm if we felt a child was not safe, and we would, sooner or later, get attention from Children's Services and perhaps the police. But, if we were to raise the alarm that a child was not enjoying life, or had an unhealthy lifestyle, or had zero prospect of achieving economic well-being, we would definitely have been ignored or perhaps even laughed at. We knew that if we didn't do this work, no one else was going to do it. With these unwanted children, we felt we were putting into practice 'Every Child Matters' in a way that no one else seemed to be equipped to do.

We looked after children in one small city in one relatively prosperous county. Such children exist all over the country. No doubt up and down the country there are other private and voluntary sector organisations doing similar work and struggling to keep their organisations afloat as 'Austerity' has bit deeper. Surely it's time we had a national approach and went beyond

---

[7] "Every child Matters" Department for Education and Skills Green Paper September 2003

paying mere lip service to mantras such as 'Every Child Matters'?

our work with children

By reading the stories you already know about the approach we took. This is not a theoretical book about psychology and behaviour but a few things need to be said.

We were often told - by parents or by members of the public in the streets - that we were doing it all wrong, that we were far too tolerant, too accepting of bad behaviour. We were told that what these children needed was the smack of firm discipline, and that we never had these problems when there was corporal punishment. It is a popular view. Obviously we rejected it. Respect4us did things in its own way.

We also rejected the behaviourist model, the basis of many school behaviour policies; essentially, it means good behaviour gets rewarded, and bad behaviour gets punished. It works with a lot of children and especially younger ones. Unfortunately, the children we were working with were not going to care about getting into trouble because they had broken the rules.

Zero tolerance policies, very fashionable as a means of turning around struggling schools, did not work with our children. In fact these policies were often the reason they were with us and not in school. Research by the American Psychological Association has shown that zero tolerance in schools "damaged relationships and decreased levels of trust and goodwill".[8] Nothing at Respect was more important to us than trust, goodwill and relationships.

---

[8] R. Skiva et al "Are zero-tolerance policies effective in the schools: An evidentiary review and recommendations" 2006 - discussed in S Roffey "The Secondary Behaviour Cookbook" 2019

We used extrinsic rewards where they were appropriate e.g. a day at the Pleasure Beach was the reward for completing the walk across Norfolk (ch6). But, of far greater value to the young person's development was the intrinsic reward, the awareness of having achieved something significant that required effort, determination and persistence. The most motivating intrinsic reward for all human beings, is having people who matter, notice what you have achieved.

So the key to unlocking the behaviour we wanted from these young people was to become people who mattered to them. There have been numerous research studies concluding that it is the quality of the adult-child relationship that matters more than anything else in effective learning and development. Having someone believe in them, and stick with them, no matter what, was the vital element in turning these young people around.

Building relationships based on trust takes time. Nothing happened overnight and we had a lot of conflict to deal with along the way. We never ignored unacceptable behaviour; it was always addressed, but never in the heat of the moment, always in situations of calm; in situations where the young person could be nudged along to recognise for themselves the hurt and damage they had caused. We always aimed to be non-confrontational. It takes two to have conflict and violence. It wasn't like we were being mugged on the street. We didn't have to fight back. We were confident in our own authority and our power but we never used it to browbeat a child into submission. Too often it is the insecure teacher who meets aggression with aggression, or the weak police officer who puts the handcuffs on rather than risking a conversation.

When there had been serious conflict we would spend a lot of time unpicking how it had developed. Normally we found that there had been a staff action that had made matters a lot worse than they had needed to be. These were children who had difficulty controlling their tempers and we could never expect them to do so. As long as our staff kept their tempers there could be no conflict.

146

A typical encounter might look like this:

"Johny I've asked you several times already. I need you to leave that video game and go and get on the bus."

"In a minute..."

"No... Now!"

Turning sharply toward me, fists clenched, "Dom, just fuck off will you and leave me alone....."

Me - half step back, open stance, hands up, palms open, head tilted, raised eyebrow...... silence.

Johny turns back to the video game. More silence.

Johny suddenly puts the controller down.

"Oh sorry, Dom, mate, look, you know I don't mean it.."

Of course not all encounters ended so easily. With all our young people it took time to develop that relationship. It took time for them to learn we were never going to react to their aggression with our own. It took time for them to learn that our lack of aggression did not mean that they could do as they pleased, time to learn that there would always be a reckoning. The reckoning might not be immediate but it would always happen as soon as the situation had calmed; and it would involve words, and the behaviour would be discussed. They also learned that we never over-reacted, we never gave up on them, and we were always there for them. In time we had their trust and respect which meant a raised eyebrow was often enough to get them to stop and self-reflect.

We each had our own style in dealing with the sort of encounter above. Women like Liz could sometimes get away with things I would never dream of risking. So the instruction to get on the minibus might have been accompanied by a tickling of the armpits, and then the games console would have been whisked away while both were in fits of giggles. Of course in training young colleagues Liz would insist that any physical contact was taboo. It takes an extraordinarily skilled and experienced practitioner to be able to judge when physical contact might be appropriate and effective. It requires an established relationship of trust where the child feels totally

147

respected as in the tickling described above, or a context of a child being so upset and distraught that the comfort of physical touch is the only way of reaching and consoling them. Our advice to young colleagues was to never overstep the touching taboo and of course never to be alone with a single child unless it was absolutely unavoidable. All the time we were making judgements about the most appropriate action and sometimes we knew we were taking risks. We protected ourselves by making sure that whenever risks were taken they were shared, discussed and logged at our end of day meeting.

Conflict was most likely to occur, not between staff and young people, but between the youngsters themselves, where neither side had the emotional control to step back from conflict. As we almost always worked in pairs we could intervene firmly, and this would be accompanied by distraction and separation of the warring parties into different rooms. One or both sides usually co-operated, relieved that blows had been prevented without any loss of face. These were great opportunities for learning, where the emotions experienced could be discussed and analysed and the other person's point of view considered. Usually there would be a shake of hands; on rare occasions, where there had been a serious breakdown in a relationship, we would consider the option of having the warring parties at the unit on different days, or perhaps one of them attending a different unit.

There were situations where one had to make a judgement call that assertive confrontation was essential. A group fight appears to be about to kick off? - step in smartly with brisk assertive body language and a complete no-nonsense stance. Most young people will take a step back, relieved that someone is in control. You might have to isolate and face down a ring leader and then you might expect to be flanked by your wingman for a show of overwhelming force. We were always on the alert and ready to cover each other's back. There was no difference in this between male and female staff; the slightest of women colleagues could be equally effective as long she was confident and assertive. The key was to use one's big weapons as sparingly and infrequently as possible. When you did deploy them you needed to be able to achieve "shock and awe".

Most of the behaviour we were dealing with on a daily basis was low level disruption and general defiance. This could often feel very personal and could require an almost superhuman effort to ignore. Being told to "fuck off", loudly, in your face, maybe with some spit included, and then to turn the other cheek, is emotionally exhausting. How did we manage it? And how did we train our staff, often very young themselves, so that they were doing it as well as the veterans?

how we trained our staff

I brought with me a vision of what I wanted Respect to be and how it could turn these children around. For years I had observed what had worked and what hadn't worked in the schools I'd served in. I had gained management skills and had learned through success and my many mistakes how to create and lead teams. Above all I brought confidence that our dream was achievable.

It was Liz who embodied all the qualities that I believed were necessary in working with troubled young people. She was a great talker but also an incredibly astute observer and listener. She would manage to identify and home in on the one tiny redeeming feature of the most obnoxious child and begin talking it up until everyone working with the child began to forget all the roughness and unpleasantness and foulness and see only the quality. Crucially, the child would often begin to start believing that he or she was not so bad after all and that he or she did have a quality that other people could admire - even love. Liz's commitment to the young people she served was total. She had none of the artificial boundaries that professional people love to create and to shelter behind. No matter what time of day or what else was going on in her life, the kids came first. She had the most amazing patience, resilience, focus and determination. She would never give up. Her approach was what we tried to replicate as the standard for all the staff.

149

We were never particularly systematic in the way we recruited our staff. Despite the low pay we never had difficulty recruiting because it was obvious to everyone that we were having fun. We poached some of our staff from our previous workplace - people that we knew were good. People would hear about Respect, come to see what we were doing, decide they wanted to join us and they were usually offered a trial. Others we stumbled across and recognised they had the skills we wanted. One or two were teachers, one an ex-headteacher, a number had worked in schools or alternative provision, some were mature with a lot of life and work experience and a few were straight out of school or college.

Those who were unknown to us always had a trial period where we assessed whether they had natural aptitude for the work. What we looked for first was evidence of understanding and sympathy with what we were trying to achieve. Did they believe that these kids could be turned around, that they were redeemable? Then we wanted to know how able they were to talk to youngsters and especially to listen to them. Could they win trust and respect, and lead without being heavy-handed? Being able to play football or having some practical skill was an added bonus. Most important of all, were they committed? The pay was rubbish and the work was hard. No one who worked with us for any length of time was doing it just because they needed a job.

We did regular formal training as a team in matters such as safeguarding and first aid but most of our training was done on the job. The key skills that were needed were absorbed through the culture and ethos of the organisation. We all accepted that we were learners and needed constant feedback from each other. Most organisations these days pay lip service to having a 'no blame' culture, but at Respect it was genuine. We wanted openness, a willingness to speak your mind about anything you were unhappy about, and with no fear of recrimination. We needed colleagues who could own their mistakes and not look to cover their backs. In this Liz and I tried to lead the way, making a point of confessing what we had got wrong and inviting criticism from the team. The following story to illustrate this is about the only occasion on which a member of staff was seriously assaulted by a young person.

Compared with all my colleagues I was old, getting a little tired and worn out, and beginning to get a little grumpy with adolescents. My young colleagues all recognised this and were very protective of me. If I seemed not to be in the right mood, they would banish me to the office to get paperwork done before I got myself into trouble. On one of these occasions, a wet afternoon, our youngsters were getting a little fractious being cooped up on indoor tasks. Getting bored with the paperwork, I came up for air and to see what was going on. I became aware of one of the older lads threatening a very irritating but much younger boy. There were plenty of staff present - I had Paul standing right in front of me - and there was no reason for me to intervene, but I said something very silly:
"If you want to pick on somebody why don't you pick on me?"
The lad gave me a hard look and got up. I thought he was heading out of the door but at the last minute he swerved towards me and shot a fist out over Paul's shoulder to land on my eye and knock me over backwards. Paul was as taken by surprise as me and was mortified that he had not protected me though it was no fault of his. I wanted to forget the incident and damage to my pride but my colleagues insisted I go to have it checked and the police be informed. Joseph took me to the hospital, the police took statements, they photographed my eye, and the boy was prosecuted. I felt terrible because I knew that I had created the situation. However, as a staff training exercise in how not to act with young people, it was invaluable. My colleagues reviewed the incident and all were able to point out to me where I had gone wrong.

The end of day staff meeting was our key tool in sharing our ethos and in developing the skills and behaviours we wanted to see in our staff. When the young people were gone and all colleagues returned to base, we sat down together and reviewed the events of the day. We talked about any incidents, walking through in detail what had happened, who had done what, and who had said what. We discussed what impact different staff actions had had. We recognised the things that had gone wrong and the interventions that were successful. Each day we all learned a little more about how to manage difficult, often crisis situations. All our staff took on this reflective practice and became really good at it. They trained themselves and each other to become truly reflective practitioners.

We expected a huge amount from them. The work was stressful, always challenging and potentially damaging to physical and especially mental health. We had to rely on colleagues to be able to read situations for themselves and then take whatever action was appropriate. There was little time during the day to give and receive instructions. Sometimes it felt like we were in the trenches and under constant fire. We had to know everybody was doing what they should and that we had each other's back. Being under fire, incidents in all directions, a teenager in your face swearing at you, turning away, while banking the memory to be dealt with later, - that requires self-control and emotional resilience. Unless at the end of the day, it's all talked through, follow-up action agreed, lessons taken on board for future practice and then everything dumped ..... unless all that happens, you are leaving a colleague to go home a possible victim of post-traumatic stress. When I went home I sometimes worried in the middle of the night about where the money was going to come from to keep my colleagues in jobs, but I never had to fret over the conflict situations I'd been in during the day, and nor did anyone else. In my many years as a teacher in mainstream schools, I had never experienced anything like this.

The other remedy for stress was laughter. It's hugely important. At our meetings there would often be great eruptions and lava flows of laughter as we replayed situations which with hindsight appeared ridiculously funny. We learned to laugh at each other, at the children and at ourselves. The joke would often continue into the days ahead and we would find ourselves spontaneously laughing when situations developed that mirrored the original cause of the merriment. All of this was vitally important in building the team spirit and camaraderie that was the best antidote to stress.

These were the ways in which Liz and I led and trained our team. In all those years I think there were only perhaps half a dozen times when I had to sit a member of staff down in private and make it clear that a behaviour was completely unacceptable and would not be tolerated. Given that we were a staff of youngsters, dropouts, mavericks, and eccentrics, this was, I thought, a pretty good record.

We got everything we asked for from the amazing people who worked for Respect4us. It was they who made the company successful and they who had an impact on the lives of thousands of young people.

a better future

Since the start of 'Austerity' in 2010 the number of children permanently excluded from school in England has increased steadily to about 8000 a year in 2017-18, and 2018-2019.[9] Obviously, a lot of money needs to be spent on these children. Now, I am not talking about billions needing to be spent. Yet, at present, billions are indeed spent by the time these children end their lives. It is spent on their poor health, the damage they do to themselves and others, the burden they put on the NHS, the welfare system, social services, the police, the courts, the prisons and probation service. Take into account also, the loss of productive output and the wasted lives, and it all amounts to many billions of pounds. Now think about this. Respect4us operated on a shoestring budget (turnover less than ¼ million pounds a year at our peak), and yet over the course of ten years we turned around thousands of children. But the way we did it,

---

[9] UK Government statistics
https://www.gov.uk/government/collections/statistics-exclusions

with no direct government funding, is simply not sustainable. Can we really not find a way of accommodating these admittedly very difficult children into our existing education system? Can we not find the extra resources needed to give them the individual care and attention they need?

I believe there should be no need for alternative provision. There is no reason why schools can't do this work themselves. They are stopped only by the artificial pressures they have been put under by all recent governments to raise academic standards. We have to start recognising that the purpose of education is far broader than the teaching and learning of traditional academic subjects. Headteachers and governing bodies need the power to be able to waive the requirement for all children to follow National Curriculum. Some schools will need specialist staff working in special units where these children's needs can be adequately met, and sometimes these units will need to be away from the main school site. However, I would argue that if many more mainstream teachers had the skills of the staff at Respect4us, most children could be kept in mainstream classrooms. It's not just about resources, the ethos has to be right, and the support for teachers has to be right. Take the pressure off, give teachers the leadership, the training, the time, the space, and the support, and the relationships will follow. It's the quality of the teacher student relationship that will keep our troubled children in school.

The National Youth Agency describes youth work as:
"working holistically with young people. It's about building resilience and character and giving young people the life skills (often totally misleadingly described as "soft") they need to live, learn, work and interact successfully with other people"[10]

The NYA is the umbrella organisation that supports and champions all youth work, yet since 2010 it has received no state funding to support its work.[11] Under 'Austerity' youth services

---

[10] https://nya.org.uk/about-us/what-we-do/
[11] https://nya.org.uk/about-us/what-we-do/

were among the first local government services to be cut. We need a properly funded national youth service with a brief to build trusted, long term relationships with the children and young people who are not getting the support they need from their own families. Youth workers would stick with their youngsters through thick and thin, supporting, advising, and advocating for them. They would open doors to a wider world, providing the physical, cultural and social experiences so many of our most deprived young people are lacking.

The problem isn't really that these youngsters fail in secondary education; their problems frequently start at birth or even in the womb. Twenty years ago the introduction of 'Sure Start' into our most deprived communities provided almost exactly what was needed. A number of studies in recent years have concluded that 'Sure Start' provided good value for money, and was beginning to make a real difference. [12] In the years up to 2010 considerable progress was made towards eradicating child poverty. If child poverty could be eliminated, there could be a role for more narrowly focused initiatives like the 'Troubled Families Programme'.

Unfortunately we have gone backwards since 2010. The funding for 'Sure Start' has been cut by two-thirds and five hundred centres have been closed. Under 'Austerity' poverty and inequality have increased alarmingly. The current 'Troubled Families Programme' will not work in the face of widespread and growing poverty. Among the stated aims of TFP is reduction of the welfare budget and getting the unemployed into jobs. Yet the majority of children in poverty are in families where the adults are in jobs that are poorly paid and insecure. [13]

---

[12] The Impact of Sure Start Local Programmes, Department for Education, Nov 2010
https://assets.publishing.service.gov.uk/government/uploads/system/uploads/attachment_data/file/182026/DFE-RR067.pdf
[13] "Learning to be poor? Poverty and the Troubled Families Programme", Child Poverty Action Group,

In her frequent and excellent briefings and reports (see Appendix 1), the Children's Commissioner, Ann Longfield catalogues the increase in inequality and disadvantage as a result of Covid-19. In "Childhood in the time of Covid" (Sept 2020) she states that even before the pandemic there were 2.2 million vulnerable children living in risky home situations in England, including nearly 800,000 children living with domestic abuse and 1.6 million living with parents with severe mental health conditions. She notes that:

"These numbers are likely to have swelled, fuelled by families locked down in close quarters for weeks and months."[14]

Calling for these vulnerable children to be prioritised, she states:

"The true measure of a society is how it treats its most vulnerable members."[15]

We need to pump money and resources into our most deprived communities, not just now during Covid, but permanently for as long as it takes to eradicate poverty. It won't cure all the problems but those remaining will be manageable. We can target mental health, alcohol and drug problems and domestic abuse. We can then do more to improve parenting and the care of the very young. We can arrest the increase in inequality and start to reverse it. Children don't need to start school months and years behind their peers and have to watch the gap grow ever wider.

At Respect4us we spent ten years trying to rescue children who shouldn't have needed rescuing. The inequality due to deprivation, poverty, neglect, abuse, poor parenting, diet, housing and lack of cultural experience shames our society. We

---

https://cpag.org.uk/news-blogs/news-listings/learning-be-poor-poverty-and-troubled-families-programme

[14] "Childhood in the Time of Covid", Children's Commissioner, September 2020

[15] "Childhood in the Time of Covid", Children's Commissioner, September 2020

have to address and remedy it if we are ever to stop wasting the lives and talents of so many of our people.

Appendix

Recent relevant reports and briefings from the Children's Commissioner

"Skipping School: Invisible Children" February 2019
"One exhausted mother described her daughter's secondary school to me as being like the Hunger Games. She, like thousands of other parents, had eventually removed her miserable
child from school – just one more effectively excluded through no fault of their own from an unforgiving school system which appears to have lost the kindness, the skill or the patience to keep them. When did school become like this?" Ann Longfield

"Exclusions from Mainstream Schools" May 2019
Raises the issue of unofficial exclusion from schools and highlights how excluded children are often the most vulnerable.

"Childhood vulnerability in England" July 2019
Estimates 2.3 million children are living with risk because of a vulnerable family background. 1.6 million of them are invisible or receiving only patchy support.

"Pass the Parcel: children posted around the care system" December 2019
The title speaks for itself.

"We're all in this together" April 2020
How vulnerable children are cut off by lockdown from their sources of support - schools, children's centres, friend and family networks, social workers and health visitors.

"Teenagers falling through the Gaps" July 2020
How Covid has greatly increased the risk of children failing in education, dropping out of school, going missing from care,

falling into crime and criminal exploitation, being unemployed as adults.

"No Way Out" August 2020
A report about homeless families living in B&Bs during the pandemic.

"Childhood in the Time of Covid" September 2020
About how all the problems for troubled children have got worse during the pandemic.

Acknowledgements

I have to thank all the amazing young people with whom I have worked during the last 45 years and who have taught me so much. Sandra Weeks was one of the very first of these to disabuse me of the notion that as a teacher I was in control of the learning process. Sandra has read and said nice things about my manuscript for which I am very grateful after all the horrible things I used to write at the bottom of her A level essays.

I am also grateful to the many other people who have read the various drafts of my manuscript and made suggestions for improvements. These included: Vanessa Bandy, Clare Barfoot, Fiona Boddington, Julie Coote, John Dent-Young, Gill Donovan, Nancy Dorner, Sylvia Ellison, Terry Haydn, Martin Kew, Emma Lowe, Mini Macdonald, Martin Phillips, Cindy Richards, Lucy Rickman, Sue Roffey, Andrew Stevens, and Peter Ward. Their encouragement gave me self-belief and kept me going.

The success of Respect4us was due to the commitment and dedication of many wonderful colleagues. These included Jason Robotham, Donna Cooper, Denise Smith, Vannessa Birchenall, Joseph Easton, Rachel Kirkham, Paul Burrows, Nicky Ives, Mark Wilkinson, Levi Lambert and very many others who worked with us for shorter periods. In writing the book I am particularly grateful to Denise Smith for her many contributions.

Respect4us was built on the skills of my co-author Liz Easton. Its existence would have been quite impossible without her. I have loved almost every minute of working with Liz over the last twenty years. Together I think we created something very special.

Setting up Respect4us involved a huge leap in the dark. If I found it easy it is because I have been married to Gill for 43 years and throughout that time she has encouraged, supported and been a ready partner in my risk-taking whatever the implications for her own comfort and security. She is everything.

Printed in Great Britain
by Amazon

81515031R00098